ACKNOWLEDGMENTS

Thanks to Digital Union

CONTENTS

AI GOVERNANCE: FOUNDATION

1.1   AI Governance Introduction

1.2   AI Ethics and Principles

1.3   Risk Management for AI Systems

1.4   AI System life cycle

1.5   AI Leadership & Governance

AI GOVERNANCE FRAMEWORK & REGULATIONS

2.1   Building Blocks of AI Governance

2.2   Data Governance for AI

2.3   Governance Frameworks

2.4   Regulatory landscapes

2.5   Public-Private Partnerships

AI GOVERNANCE IN PRACTICE

3.1   Navigating the Age of AI

3.2   Tools for Responsible AI

3.3   Case Studies of Effective Governance

3.4   Human Factor

3.5   Emerging Technologies and Future Challenges

INTRODUCTION

Today, we are witnessing another seismic shift. **While software has eaten the world, AI is now eating the Universe**. Artificial Intelligence is not just another technological advancement, but a paradigm shifts in how leaders lead and how we think. AI's ability to analyze vast amounts of data, learn from patterns, and make decisions with unprecedented speed and accuracy is reshaping industries at an extraordinary pace. This is not just disruption; it is reinvention.

The future of AI is one where businesses will no longer compete solely on products or services but on how effectively they leverage AI to innovate, adapt, and deliver value. AI will redefine industries, create new markets, and unlock possibilities previously unimaginable. From healthcare to finance, manufacturing to education, AI's transformative potential is boundless, making it the cornerstone of future business.

However, with great power comes great responsibility. As AI becomes deeply integrated into every aspect of our lives, the need for ethical considerations, trustworthiness, and alignment with human values becomes paramount. Organizations must not only adopt AI but do so in a way that ensures it serves the greater good and builds trust with stakeholders.

WHY AI IS IMPORTANT

AI has rapidly become one of the most transformative forces of the 21st century. It is reshaping industries, redefining workflows, and revolutionizing the way we live and work. To understand its significance, we must delve into its potential to:

- **Automate Complex Tasks:** AI can handle intricate and repetitive tasks with precision, allowing humans to focus on creative and strategic activities.

- **Enhance Decision-Making:** Through advanced data analytics and predictive modeling, AI empowers businesses to make informed, real-time decisions.

- **Personalize Experiences:** AI-driven personalization tailors products and services to individual preferences, enhancing customer satisfaction and loyalty.

- **Drive Innovation:** AI enables breakthroughs in fields like healthcare, finance, education, and entertainment, opening doors to possibilities previously thought unattainable.

AI TRANSFORMING INDUSTRIES

AI is changing the landscape of various industries. Some examples include:

- **Healthcare:** AI-powered diagnostic tools, virtual health assistants, and robotic surgeries are improving patient outcomes and reducing costs.
- **Finance:** Automated trading algorithms, fraud detection systems, and customer service chatbots are enhancing efficiency and security.
- **Manufacturing:** Smart factories leverage AI for predictive maintenance, supply chain optimization, and quality control.
- **Retail:** AI enhances inventory management, optimizes pricing strategies, and offers personalized shopping experiences.
- **Education:** Adaptive learning platforms powered by AI tailor content delivery to individual learning styles and paces.

A Brief History of AI and Its Evolution

Early Beginnings

- **1950s:** Alan Turing proposes the Turing Test to assess machine intelligence.
- **1956:** The term "Artificial Intelligence" is coined at the Dartmouth Conference, marking the birth of AI as a

field of study.

Growth and Challenges

- **1960s-70s:** Early AI programs like ELIZA and SHRDLU demonstrate basic natural language processing capabilities.

- **AI Winters:** Periods of reduced funding and interest due to overhyped expectations and slow progress.

Modern Resurgence

- **2000s-Present:** Advances in computing power, big data, and machine learning algorithms fuel AI's growth. Breakthroughs in neural networks, natural language processing, and computer vision pave the way for real-world applications.

THE IMPERATIVE FOR AI GOVERNANCE

- Artificial Intelligence (AI) is transforming every aspect of human society—from healthcare and education to finance, security, and governance. Its rapid advancement brings unprecedented opportunities but also significant risks, including ethical dilemmas, biases, job displacement, and even existential threats if left unchecked. As AI systems grow more autonomous and influential, the need for robust **AI**

Governance becomes not just important but essential.

- This book, *AI Governance: Navigating the Future of Artificial Intelligence*, explores the frameworks, policies, and ethical considerations required to ensure that AI development aligns with human values, societal well-being, and global stability. We examine the challenges and opportunities in regulating AI, the role of governments and corporations, and the international cooperation needed to prevent misuse while fostering innovation.

WHY AI GOVERNANCE IS KEY FOR THE WORLD: CHALLENGES AND SOLUTIONS

THE CRITICAL NEED FOR AI GOVERNANCE

Artificial Intelligence (AI) is advancing at an unprecedented pace, reshaping economies, societies, and global power structures. While AI offers immense benefits—from medical breakthroughs to climate solutions—it also introduces risks that, if left unregulated, could lead to societal harm, economic instability, and even existential threats.

AI GOVERNANCE—the framework of policies, ethics, and

regulations guiding AI development and deployment—is essential to ensure that AI serves humanity's best interests rather than undermining them. Without governance, AI could exacerbate inequality, erode privacy, destabilize democracies, and create uncontrollable autonomous systems.

Key Challenges Posed by Unregulated AI

1. ETHICAL AND BIAS CONCERNS

- **Problem:** AI systems can perpetuate and amplify human biases in hiring, law enforcement, and lending (e.g., facial recognition misidentifying minorities, AI hiring tools favoring male candidates).
- **Governance Solution:**
    - Mandate **bias audits** and **diverse training datasets**.
    - Enforce **algorithmic transparency** to detect and correct discriminatory patterns.

2. PRIVACY AND SURVEILLANCE RISKS

- **Problem:** AI enables mass data collection, deepfake manipulation, and intrusive surveillance (e.g., China's social credit system, unauthorized facial recognition).
- **Governance Solution:**
    - Strengthen **data protection laws** (e.g., GDPR,

AI-specific privacy regulations).

- o Ban or restrict **real-time mass surveillance** without judicial oversight.

3. AUTONOMOUS WEAPONS AND WARFARE

- **Problem:** AI-powered drones and autonomous weapons could lead to uncontrolled warfare, accidental escalations, and loss of human oversight.
- **Governance Solution:**
  - o International treaties (like the **UN's call for a ban on lethal autonomous weapons**).
  - o Require **human-in-the-loop controls** for military AI.

4. JOB DISPLACEMENT AND ECONOMIC INEQUALITY

- **Problem:** AI automation threatens millions of jobs, potentially widening the wealth gap.
- **Governance Solution:**
  - o Implement **AI taxation** (e.g., robot tax) to fund reskilling programs.
  - o Promote **human-AI collaboration** rather than full automation.

5. MISINFORMATION AND AI-GENERATED DECEPTION

- **Problem:** AI can generate hyper-realistic deepfakes, fake news, and propaganda, undermining trust in media and democracy.
- **Governance Solution:**

- o Require **watermarking for AI-generated content.**
- o Hold platforms accountable for **algorithmic amplification of disinformation.**

6. EXISTENTIAL AND ALIGNMENT RISKS

- **Problem:** Advanced AI systems could act unpredictably if their goals are misaligned with human values (e.g., an AI optimizing for efficiency at the cost of safety).

- **Governance Solution:**
  - o **Strict safety protocols** for AI development (e.g., OpenAI's alignment research).
  - o **Global cooperation** to prevent an AI arms race (similar to nuclear non-proliferation).

Key Challenges in AI & How Governance Helps

Challenge	Governance Solutions
1. AI Bias & Discrimination	Enforce fairness and transparency in AI decision-making (e.g., anti-bias audits, explainability standards).
2. Data Privacy & Security	Implement strict data protection laws (GDPR, AI Act) to regulate AI-driven surveillance and data misuse.
3. AI Accountability & Ethics	Require AI developers to explain AI decisions, ensuring human oversight and responsibility.
4. Autonomous AI & Safety Risks	Set legal frameworks to regulate high-risk AI systems like self-driving cars and autonomous weapons.
5. AI's Impact on Jobs & Economy	Create policies for AI-driven workforce transitions, reskilling programs, and universal basic income discussions.
6. AI in National Security &	Establish international AI agreements to prevent AI weaponization and

Cybersecurity	cyber threats.
7. Deepfakes & Misinformation	Regulate AI-generated content, enforce digital authenticity standards, and combat AI-driven misinformation.
8. AI Monopolies & Power Concentration	Introduce AI competition laws to prevent big tech from monopolizing AI innovation.

1. REGULATORY FRAMEWORKS AND STANDARDS

- **National Laws:** Countries must adopt AI regulations (e.g., **EU AI Act**, **U.S. AI Executive Orders**) to set safety and ethical standards.
- **Global Coordination:** International bodies (UN, OECD, G20) should harmonize AI policies to prevent regulatory fragmentation.

2. CORPORATE ACCOUNTABILITY

- Tech companies must adopt **ethical AI principles**, establish **AI review boards**, and ensure **transparency in AI decision-making**.
- Example: Google's **AI Principles** ban AI for weapons and require fairness assessments.

3. PUBLIC PARTICIPATION AND TRANSPARENCY

- Governments and firms should engage **civil society, ethicists, and marginalized groups** in AI policy discussions.

- Open-source AI audits and **third-party oversight** can increase accountability.

4. ADAPTIVE AND PROACTIVE GOVERNANCE

- AI evolves rapidly, so governance must be **flexible—** using **sandbox testing** and iterative policy updates.
- **Precautionary measures** (e.g., pausing risky AI research) should be enforced when necessary.

AI GOVERNANCE AS A GLOBAL IMPERATIVE

AI is too powerful to remain unchecked. Without governance, its risks could outweigh its benefits, leading to societal fractures, loss of privacy, and even catastrophic outcomes. However, with **strong, ethical, and adaptive AI governance**, we can harness AI's potential while safeguarding democracy, human rights, and global stability.

The Age of AI: Power, Promise, and Peril

The Age of AI: Power, Promise, and Peril" explores the transformative potential of artificial intelligence, highlighting its benefits, risks, and ethical considerations. Here are some key themes you could incorporate into your book:

1. **The Power of AI**
    o AI's ability to revolutionize industries like healthcare, education, and transportation.
    o Enhancing productivity and decision-making through machine learning and automation.

o The role of AI in addressing global challenges, such as climate change and resource management.

2. **The Promise of AI**

   o Opportunities for innovation and economic growth.

   o Improving quality of life through personalized services and accessibility.

   o AI's potential to democratize knowledge and bridge societal gaps.

3. **The Peril of AI**

   o Ethical dilemmas, such as bias, privacy concerns, and surveillance.

   o Risks of misuse, including autonomous weapons and misinformation.

   o The challenge of ensuring accountability and transparency in AI systems.

4. **Balancing Power, Promise, and Peril**

   o The importance of responsible AI governance to mitigate risks.

   o Developing global frameworks and regulations to ensure ethical AI use.

   o Encouraging collaboration between governments, industries, and academia.

THE CHOICE IS CLEAR: EITHER WE GOVERN AI, OR IT WILL GOVERN US. THE TIME TO ACT IS NOW.

Case Studies in AI Ethics

MICROSOFT'S TAY CHATBOT (2016)

- **What Happened:** Tay, an AI chatbot launched on Twitter, was designed to learn from user interactions. Within hours, it began generating offensive and inappropriate content due to malicious inputs from users.

- **Governance Failures:** Lack of safeguards against harmful content and insufficient testing of the chatbot's resilience to adversarial behavior.

- **Lessons Learned:** The importance of robust content moderation, ethical oversight, and pre-deployment testing to prevent misuse.

2. AMAZON'S RECRUITMENT AI (2018)

- **What Happened:** Amazon developed an AI tool to screen job applicants, but it showed bias against female candidates because it was trained on historical data reflecting gender imbalances in the tech industry.

- **Governance Failures:** Failure to ensure unbiased training data and lack of regular audits to detect discriminatory patterns.

- **Lessons Learned:** The need for diverse and representative datasets, as well as continuous monitoring to mitigate algorithmic bias.

3. UBER'S SELF-DRIVING CAR ACCIDENT (2018)

- **What Happened:** An Uber self-driving car struck and killed a pedestrian in Arizona. The AI system failed to identify the pedestrian as a hazard in time to avoid the collision.
- **Governance Failures:** Inadequate safety protocols, insufficient testing in real-world scenarios, and lack of accountability mechanisms.
- **Lessons Learned:** The critical need for rigorous safety standards, transparent testing processes, and clear accountability in autonomous systems.

4. APPLE CARD GENDER BIAS (2019)

- **What Happened:** Apple's credit card algorithm was accused of gender bias when it offered significantly lower credit limits to women compared to men, even when they had similar financial profiles.
- **Governance Failures:** Lack of transparency in the algorithm's decision-making process and insufficient checks for discriminatory outcomes.
- **Lessons Learned:** The importance of explainability in AI systems and proactive measures to identify and eliminate bias.

5. CLEARVIEW AI'S FACIAL RECOGNITION CONTROVERSY (2020)

- **What Happened:** Clearview AI faced backlash for scraping billions of images from social media without consent to build its facial recognition database, which was then sold to law enforcement agencies.

- **Governance Failures:** Violation of privacy rights, lack of informed consent, and absence of ethical guidelines for data usage.

- **Lessons Learned:** The necessity of adhering to privacy laws, obtaining user consent, and establishing ethical boundaries for data collection.

6. TESLA'S AUTOPILOT CRASHES (ONGOING)

- **What Happened:** Tesla's Autopilot system has been involved in multiple accidents, raising concerns about its reliability and the company's marketing of the feature as "self-driving."

- **Governance Failures:** Over-reliance on users to monitor the system, lack of clear communication about its limitations, and insufficient regulatory oversight.

- **Lessons Learned:** The need for clear labeling of AI capabilities, user education, and stricter regulatory frameworks for autonomous technologies.

AI Ethics & Principles

As artificial intelligence becomes increasingly embedded in society, ethical considerations must guide its development and deployment. Without strong ethical frameworks, AI risks amplifying biases, eroding privacy, and even threatening human autonomy. This chapter explores **core AI ethics principles**, global guidelines, and practical approaches to ensure AI aligns with human values.

Definition: Ethical AI refers to artificial intelligence systems designed and deployed in ways that respect moral principles, human rights, and societal well-being. It ensures AI does not harm individuals or groups and aligns with widely accepted ethical norms.

KEY ASPECTS OF ETHICAL AI:

✓ **Human-Centric Design** – AI should augment, not replace, human decision-making.

✓ **Moral Alignment** – AI must adhere to ethical frameworks (e.g., fairness, justice, non-maleficence).

✓ **Societal Impact Assessment** – Evaluates long-term consequences on communities.

Example:

- An **AI hiring tool** that avoids gender/racial bias is *ethical*.

- A **deepfake generator** used for misinformation

is *unethical.*

FOUNDATIONAL AI ETHICS PRINCIPLES

1.1 Transparency (Explainability)

- **Definition:** AI systems should provide clear, understandable reasoning for their decisions.
- **Why It Matters:**
  - Ensures accountability (e.g., if an AI denies a loan, the applicant should know why).
  - Builds public trust in AI applications (medical diagnosis, legal judgments).
- **Implementation:**
  - **Explainable AI (XAI) techniques** (decision trees, attention maps in neural networks).
  - **Regulatory mandates** (EU AI Act requires transparency for high-risk AI).

1.2 Fairness & Bias Mitigation

- **Definition:** AI must avoid discrimination based on race, gender, age, or other protected attributes.
- **Why It Matters:**
  - Prevents harm (e.g., biased hiring algorithms, racially skewed facial recognition).
  - Ensures equitable access to AI benefits.
- **Implementation:**
  - **Bias audits** (IBM's Fairness 360 Toolkit, Google's Responsible AI practices).

- o **Diverse training datasets** to reflect real-world populations.

1.3 Privacy & Data Protection

- **Definition:** AI must respect user data rights and minimize surveillance risks.
- **Why It Matters:**
  - o Prevents misuse (e.g., mass surveillance, deepfake exploitation).
  - o Complies with laws like **GDPR** and **CCPA.**
- **Implementation:**
  - o **Federated learning** (AI trains on decentralized data without raw access).
  - o **Differential privacy** (adding noise to datasets to protect identities).

1.4 Accountability & Responsibility

- **Definition:** Clear lines of responsibility when AI causes harm.
- **Why It Matters:**
  - o Determines liability (e.g., who is at fault if a self-driving car crashes?).
  - o Encourages rigorous testing and risk assessment.
- **Implementation:**
  - o **AI incident databases** (Partnership on AI's registry of failures).
  - o **Legal frameworks** assigning liability to

developers, deployers, or users.

1.5 Safety & Robustness

- **Definition:** AI must function reliably under uncertain conditions.

- **Why It Matters:**
  - o Prevents catastrophic failures (e.g., AI-powered stock market crashes).
  - o Ensures AI behaves predictably in critical systems (healthcare, aviation).

- **Implementation:**
  - o **Red-teaming** (stress-testing AI for vulnerabilities).
  - o **Fail-safe mechanisms** (e.g., automatic shutdowns for erratic behavior).

1.6 Human Autonomy & Oversight

- **Definition:** Humans must retain ultimate control over AI decisions.

- **Why It Matters:**
  - o Prevents unchecked AI power (e.g., autonomous weapons, AI judges).
  - o Aligns AI with human moral reasoning.

- **Implementation:**
  - o **Human-in-the-loop (HITL)** systems for high-stakes decisions.
  - o **Ethical review boards** for AI deployments in sensitive fields.

GLOBAL AI ETHICS FRAMEWORKS

2.1 The EU's Ethics Guidelines for Trustworthy AI

- **Key Principles:**
    - Human agency and oversight.
    - Technical robustness and safety.
    - Privacy and data governance.
    - Transparency.
    - Diversity, non-discrimination, and fairness.
    - Societal and environmental well-being.
    - Accountability.

2.2 OECD AI Principles

- **Adopted by 50+ countries**, including the U.S. and EU:
    1. AI should benefit people and the planet.
    2. AI systems should respect human rights and fairness.
    3. AI must be transparent and explainable.
    4. AI should be robust, secure, and safe.
    5. Organizations developing AI must be accountable.

2.3 IEEE's Ethically Aligned Design

- **Focus:** Engineers should prioritize ethical considerations in AI development.
- **Key Recommendations:**
    - Embed ethical values into system design.
    - Prioritize long-term societal impacts over short-

term profits.

2.4 China's AI Ethics Principles

- **Emphasis on:**
    - o "Controllable and reliable" AI.
    - o Social stability (aligned with state interests).
    - o Contrasts with Western individualism (collectivist approach).

IMPLEMENTING AI ETHICS IN PRACTICE

3.1 Corporate AI Ethics Boards

- **Examples:**
    - o **Google's AI Principles** (banning AI for weapons, avoiding bias).
    - o **Microsoft's AETHER Committee** (Advancing AI Ethics).
- **Best Practices:**
    - o Independent oversight (not just PR).
    - o Public transparency in decision-making.

3.2 Government Regulations

- **EU AI Act (2025):**
    - o Bans certain AI uses (social scoring, manipulative AI).
    - o Requires risk assessments for high-stakes AI.
- **U.S. AI Bill of Rights (2022):**
    - o Protects against algorithmic discrimination.
    - o Ensures data privacy.

3.3 Public Advocacy & Whistleblowing

- **Case Study:**
  - o **Frances Haugen's Facebook leaks** showed algorithmic harms.
- **Tools for Accountability:**
  - o **AI audit frameworks** (Algorithmic Justice League).
  - o **Whistleblower protections** for tech employees.

CHALLENGES IN IMPLEMENTATION

- Bias in AI – Historical data can reinforce discrimination.
- Explainability vs. Performance – Complex AI (e.g., deep learning) is often a "black box."
- Regulatory Fragmentation – Different countries have conflicting AI laws.
- Corporate Resistance – Profit motives may override ethical concerns

THE FUTURE OF ETHICAL AI

AI ethics is not a luxury—it's a necessity to prevent harm and ensure AI serves humanity. The principles outlined here must evolve alongside AI's rapid advancements. **The choice is clear: Either we shape AI with ethics, or unethical AI will shape us.**

Call to Action:

- **For Developers:** Build ethics into AI from the start.
- **For Policymakers:** Enforce strict but adaptable regulations.
- **For Citizens:** Demand transparency and accountability.

CASE STUDY COMPARISON: ETHICAL AI IN PRACTICE

CHATGPT (RESPONSIBLE AI) VS. PREDICTIVE POLICING AI (BIASED LAW ENFORCEMENT TOOL)

This case study compares two real-world AI applications—one designed with ethical safeguards (ChatGPT) and a predictive policing system that amplified societal biases—to illustrate the importance of Responsible AI principles.

1. CHATGPT: A (MOSTLY) RESPONSIBLE AI MODEL
BACKGROUND:

- Developed by OpenAI as a general-purpose conversational AI
- Designed with multiple layers of ethical safeguards

POSITIVE ETHICAL PRACTICES:

✓ **Content Moderation** – Implements filters for harmful

content

✓ **Transparency Efforts** – Publishes model limitations and safety approaches

✓ **User Controls** – Provides opt-out mechanisms for data privacy

✓ **Bias Reduction** – Ongoing work to minimize stereotypical outputs

ETHICAL CHALLENGES:

- Occasional factual inaccuracies ("hallucinations")
- Copyright concerns regarding training data
- Potential workforce displacement impacts

WHY IT REPRESENTS RESPONSIBLE AI:

- Proactive ethical framework implementation
- Willingness to address shortcomings
- Engagement with stakeholders

2. PREDICTIVE POLICING AI: A CAUTIONARY TALE

BACKGROUND:

- Marketed to law enforcement agencies as a crime prevention tool
- Used machine learning to generate patrol ·recommendations

Amplified Racial Biases

• Trained on historically biased arrest records

• Systematically targeted marginalized neighborhoods

Lack of Accountability

• Proprietary "black box" algorithm

• No meaningful oversight mechanisms

Real-World Harm

• Increased over-policing in minority communities

• Eroded public trust in law enforcement

• Eventually discontinued by multiple police departments

Root Causes of Failure:

• Failure to audit for discriminatory impacts

• Absence of community consultation

• Profit-driven deployment without ethical review

3. KEY COMPARATIVE TAKEAWAYS

Ethical Factor	*ChatGPT*	*Predictive Policing AI*
Bias Mitigation	Active efforts	Reinforced systemic bias
Transparency	Public disclosures	Opaque operations
Accountability	Responsive to	No redress

	feedback	mechanisms
Benefit/Risk Ratio	Generally positive	Net harmful outcomes
Regulatory Compliance	Proactive adherence	Minimal oversight

4. CRITICAL LESSONS FOR AI GOVERNANCE

1. **Pre-Deployment Audits Are Essential**
   - Must test for discriminatory impacts before real-world use

2. **Transparency Enables Accountability**
   - Black-box systems in sensitive applications create unacceptable risks

3. **Stakeholder Inclusion Matters**
   - Affected communities must have input on high-stakes AI deployments

4. **Profit Motives Require Balancing**
   - Commercial AI in public sector needs strong safeguards

5. RECOMMENDATIONS FOR POLICYMAKERS

✓ Mandate algorithmic impact assessments for public safety AI

✓ Require public transparency reporting for government AI systems

✓ Establish independent oversight boards for law enforcement AI

✓ Create liability frameworks for harmful AI applications

Risk Management & AI System

AI RISK MANAGEMENT: STRATEGIES FOR SAFE AND RESPONSIBLE AI SYSTEMS

1. Understanding AI Risks

AI systems introduce unique risks that require proactive management:

Key AI Risk Categories

Risk Type	Examples	Potential Impact
Technical Risks	Model bias, adversarial attacks, system failures	Unfair decisions, security breaches
Ethical Risks	Privacy violations, discrimination, misuse	Loss of trust, legal penalties
Operational Risks	Poor data quality, lack of human oversight	System failures, financial losses
Strategic Risks	AI arms race, regulatory non-compliance	Reputation damage, market exclusion
Existential Risks	Superintelligence misalignment	Catastrophic societal harm

2. AI RISK MANAGEMENT FRAMEWORK

A structured approach to identifying, assessing, and mitigating AI risks:

Step 1: Risk Identification

- **Conduct AI impact assessments** (e.g., EU AI Act's

risk classifications)

- **Map failure modes** (e.g., bias in training data, edge-case vulnerabilities)

Step 2: Risk Assessment

- **Severity:** How harmful could the risk be? (e.g., deepfake election interference > chatbot errors)
- **Likelihood:** Probability of occurrence (e.g., biased outputs in unchecked models)

Step 3: Risk Mitigation

Risk	Mitigation Strategy
Bias & Fairness	Bias audits (IBM Fairness 360), diverse datasets
Security Attacks	Adversarial training, input sanitization
Privacy Breaches	Federated learning, differential privacy
Misalignment	Human-in-the-loop controls, reward modeling
Regulatory,Non-Compliance	Alignment with GDPR, EU AI Act, ISO 42001

Step 4: Monitoring & Response

- **Real-time monitoring:** Detect drift in model performance (e.g., Fiddler AI, WhyLabs)
- **Incident response plans:** For AI failures (e.g., shutdown protocols for harmful outputs)

3. AI SYSTEM SAFETY BY DESIGN

Core Principles for Safe AI Systems

1. **Transparency**
   - Explainable AI (XAI) techniques (SHAP, LIME)
   - Documentation of training data and decision logic

2. **Robustness**
   - Stress-testing under extreme conditions (e.g., NVIDIA's "Break-It" testing)
   - Fail-safe mechanisms (e.g., automatic shutdowns for erratic behavior)

3. **Accountability**
   - Clear ownership of AI decisions (e.g., EU's proposed AI liability rules)
   - Audit trails for high-stakes AI (healthcare, criminal justice)

4. **Human Oversight**
   - "Human-in-the-loop" for critical decisions (e.g., medical diagnosis AI)
   - Right to appeal automated decisions (e.g., loan rejections)

4. CASE STUDIES IN AI RISK MANAGEMENT

Success: OpenAI's GPT-4 Safety Measures

- **Mitigations:**

- o **Pre-deployment red-teaming** (hacker-style testing)
- o **Refusal protocols** for harmful requests
- o **Continuous monitoring** for misuse

Failure: Tesla Autopilot Crashes

- **Root Causes:**
  - o Overreliance on vision-only AI (missed edge cases)
  - o Inadequate driver monitoring
- **Lessons:**
  - o Need for **multi-sensor redundancy** in safety-critical AI
  - o

✓ **Proactive risk assessment** is cheaper than post-failure fixes

✓ **"Safety by design"** beats bolt-on solutions

✓ **Regulation is coming** – compliant AI systems will have a market advantage

---

AI Risk Management Tools: A Comprehensive Guide

AI risk management tools help organizations **identify, assess, monitor, and mitigate** risks associated with AI systems.

Below is a categorized list of **leading tools and frameworks** for AI governance, bias detection, security, and compliance.

1. AI GOVERNANCE & COMPLIANCE TOOLS

These tools help organizations align AI systems with regulations (GDPR, EU AI Act, NIST AI RMF).

Tool	Provider	Key Features
IBM watsonx.governance	IBM	- Monitors AI models for bias/drift - Audit trails for compliance
Fairly	Holistic AI	- AI risk scoring - GDPR/EU AI Act compliance checks
SAS Model Manager	SAS	- Lifecycle tracking of AI models - Compliance documentation
Google Responsible AI Toolkit	Google	- Bias/fairness evaluation - Explainability dashboards

Use Case:

- A bank uses **watsonx.governance** to ensure its loan-approval AI complies with anti-discrimination laws.

2. BIAS & FAIRNESS DETECTION TOOLS

Detect and mitigate bias in training data and AI outputs.

Tool	Provider	Key Features
Aequitas	University of Chicago	- Open-source bias audit tool - Works with Python
Fairlearn	Microsoft	- Measures fairness metrics (demographic parity)
AI Fairness 360 (AIF360)	IBM	- 70+ fairness metrics - Bias mitigation algorithms
TensorFlow Fairness Indicators	Google	- Bias visualization for ML models

Use Case:

- A hiring firm uses **Aequitas** to check if its AI recruitment tool favors male candidates.

3. AI SECURITY & ADVERSARIAL TESTING TOOLS

Protect AI models from hacking, data poisoning, and

adversarial attacks.

Tool	*Provider*	*Key Features*
Counterfit	Microsoft	Automated adversarial attack simulation
Adversarial Robustness Toolbox (ART)	IBM	Defends against model evasion attacks
Robust Intelligence	Robust Intelligence	Stress-tests AI models pre-deployment
DeepArmor	Trend Micro	Detects malicious AI-generated content

Use Case:

- A self-driving car company uses **ART** to test if its vision AI can be fooled by fake road signs.

4. AI EXPLAINABILITY & TRANSPARENCY TOOLS

Make AI decisions interpretable for regulators and end-users.

Tool	Provider	Key Features
SHAP(SHapley Additive exPlanations)	Open-source	- Explains model predictions - Works with

		Python
LIME(Local Interpretable Model-agnostic Explanations)	Open-source	- Simplifies complex AI decisions
Fiddler AI	Fiddler Labs	- Monitors model behavior in production
WhyLabs	AWS	- Detects data drift in real-time

Use Case:

- A hospital uses **SHAP** to explain why an AI diagnostic tool flagged a patient as high-risk.

5. AI RISK ASSESSMENT FRAMEWORKS

Structured methodologies for evaluating AI risks.

Framework	Provider	Key Features
NIST AI Risk Management Framework (RMF)	U.S. Government	- Voluntary standards for trustworthy AI
ISO 42001 (AI Management System)	ISO	- Global standard for AI governance
EU AI Act Compliance Toolkit	EU Commission	- Checks for high-risk AI

		requirements
OECD AI Principles Assessment	OECD	- Self-assessment for ethical AI

Use Case:

- A fintech startup uses **NIST AI RMF** to assess risks before launching a fraud-detection AI.

6. AI INCIDENT MONITORING & RESPONSE

Track AI failures and implement corrective actions.

Tool	Provider	Key Features
MLflow	Databricks	Logs AI model performance/issues
Arthur AI	Arthur	Detects model drift and anomalies
Monitaur	Monitaur	Blockchain-based AI audit trails

Use Case:

- An e-commerce platform uses **Arthur AI** to detect when its recommendation engine starts showing biased product suggestions.

CHOOSING THE RIGHT AI RISK MANAGEMENT TOOL

Need	Recommended Tool
Regulatory Compliance	IBM watsonx.governance, Fairly
Bias Detection	Aequitas, AIF360
Security Testing	Counterfit, ART

Explainability	SHAP, Fiddler AI
Risk Assessment	NIST AI RMF, ISO 42001

✓ **Governance tools** (e.g., watsonx) ensure compliance with laws like the EU AI Act.

✓ **Bias detection tools** (e.g., Fairlearn) prevent discriminatory AI outcomes.

✓ **Security tools** (e.g., ART) protect against adversarial attacks.

✓ **Explainability tools** (e.g., SHAP) build trust in AI decisions.

AI RISK MANAGEMENT ASSESSMENT TEMPLATE

Project: [AI System Name]
Organization: [Your Company]
Date: [MM/DD/YYYY]
Prepared by: [Your Name]

---

1. Executive Summary

Briefly describe the AI system, its purpose, and key risks identified.

Example:

"This assessment evaluates [AI System Name], a [describe function, e.g.,

'facial recognition tool for security']. Risks are quantified using likelihood/impact scores, and mitigation plans are prioritized based on severity."

2. Risk Identification & Quantification

Use a **1–5 scale** *(1=Low, 5=High) to score likelihood and impact. Calculate* **Risk Score = Likelihood × Impact**.

Risk Category	Risk Description	Likelihood (1–5)	Impact (1–5)	Risk Score (L×I)	Priority (H/M/L)
Bias & Fairness	Gender bias in hiring recommendations	4	5	**20 (High)**	Critical
Security	Adversarial attacks corrupting model	3	5	**15 (High)**	Critical
Privacy	Training data leaks PII	3	4	**12 (Medium)**	High
Compliance	Non-compliance with EU AI Act	2	5	**10 (Medium)**	High
Operational	System downtime (>2 hrs/month)	4	3	**12 (Medium)**	Moderate

Priority Thresholds:

- **Critical (15–25):** Immediate action required.

- **High (8–14):** Mitigate within 3 months.

- **Moderate/Low (1–7):** Monitor or accept risk.

3. Risk Mitigation Actions

For each high/critical risk, specify actions, owners, and deadlines.

Risk (Score)	Mitigation Action	Owner	Deadline	Status
Bias in hiring (20)	1. Audit training data for gender skew. 2. Implement IBM Fairness 360 toolkit.	Data Science Team	MM/DD/YYYY	[✓/○/✗]
Adversarial attacks (15)	1. Conduct penetration testing. 2. Deploy adversarial training (e.g., CleverHans).	Security Team	MM/DD/YYYY	[✓/○/✗]
PII leakage (12)	1. Anonymize datasets. 2. Restrict access with role-based	Privacy Officer	MM/DD/YYYY	[✓/○/✗]

controls.			

4. Monitoring & Controls

Define metrics and frequency for ongoing risk tracking.

Risk	Monitoring Metric	Frequency	Threshold for Alert
Bias & Fairness	Disparate impact ratio (<0.8 or >1.25)	Monthly	Metric out of range
Security	# Detected adversarial attempts	Weekly	>5 attempts/month
Privacy	# Unauthorized data access incidents	Quarterly	Any incident

5. Contingency Plans

For critical risks, outline emergency responses.

Example – Model Bias Incident:

- **Step 1:** Pull biased model from production immediately.
- **Step 2:** Notify legal/comms teams for public response.
- **Step 3:** Retrain model with debiased dataset (ETA: 2 weeks).

6. Conclusion

Summarize key risks, actions, and next steps.

"Critical risks (scores ≥15) require immediate mitigation, starting with [Action 1] and [Action 2]. Medium risks will be addressed per the timeline above. Quarterly reviews will ensure compliance."

Project: *SecureFace 2.0 (Facial Recognition for Airport Security)*

Organization: *SecureFace Inc.*

Date: *March 15, 2024*

Prepared by: *Chief AI Officer*

1. EXECUTIVE SUMMARY

"SecureFace 2.0 is an AI-powered facial recognition system used at airports for passenger verification. This assessment identifies high risks of racial bias and adversarial attacks, scoring them as critical (15+). Mitigation includes bias audits and model hardening."

2. RISK IDENTIFICATION & QUANTIFICATION

Risk Category	Risk Description	Likelihood (1–5)	Impact (1–5)	Risk Score (L×I)	Priority

Bias & Fairness	Higher false negatives for dark-skinned users	4	5	2 0	Critic al
Security	Adversarial patches trick the system (e.g., printed glasses)	3	5	1 5	Critic al
Privacy	Passenger data leaked to third parties	3	4	1 2	High
Compliance	Violates EU AI Act (banned real-time biometrics)	2	5	1 0	High
Operation al	**System crashes during peak hours (2 incidents/mont h)**	**4**	**3**	**1 2**	**Mod erate**

3. RISK MITIGATION ACTIONS

Risk (Score)	Action Plan	Owner	Dea dline	S tatus
Bias (20)	1. Retrain model with MORPH dataset (diverse skin tones). 2. Integrate *FairFace* bias detector.	AI Ethics Team	Apri l 30, 2024	✅
Adversaria l (15)	1. Deploy *CleverHans* adversari al training.	Cybersec urity Team	May 15, 2024	◯

	2. Test with "fooling glasses" attacks.			
Privacy (12)	1. Encrypt passenger data in transit/rest. 2. Conduct GDPR compliance audit.	Data Privacy Officer	June 1, 2024	✗

4. MONITORING & CONTROLS

Risk	Metric	Frequency	Alert Threshold
Bias & Fairness	False Negative Rate by skin tone	Weekly	>5% disparity
Security	Adversarial bypass attempts	Daily	>1 attempt/week
Privacy	Unauthorized data access incidents	Monthly	Any incident

5. CONTINGENCY PLAN

Example Incident: *Bias scandal reported in media (July 2023).*

- Immediate Response:
    1. Disable SecureFace 2.0 at affected airports.
    2. Issue public apology and corrective timeline.
- Long-Term Fix:
    - Partner with *NIST* to certify bias mitigation.

AI System Life Cycle

The **System Life Cycle** is a structured framework that guides the development, deployment, and maintenance of systems, including AI systems. It is **invaluable** because it ensures that systems are built efficiently, meet business needs, and deliver long-term value. Below, I'll explain **why the System Life Cycle is valuable**, its benefits, and how it applies to AI systems.

WHY THE SYSTEM LIFE CYCLE IS VALUABLE

The System Life Cycle provides a structured, repeatable, and disciplined approach to building and managing systems. It ensures that systems are developed with clear objectives, meet user requirements, and are maintainable over time. Here's why it's valuable:

1. Ensures Alignment with Business Goals

- The System Life Cycle ensures that systems are designed to solve real business problems and deliver measurable value.

- **Example**: An AI system for fraud detection is developed to reduce financial losses, directly aligning with the company's goal of improving profitability.

2. Reduces Risks

- By following a structured process, organizations can

identify and mitigate risks early in the development process.

- **Example**: Conducting feasibility studies during the Planning phase helps identify potential challenges before investing heavily in development.

3. Improves Efficiency

- The System Life Cycle breaks down complex projects into manageable phases, making it easier to allocate resources and track progress.
- **Example**: Using Agile methodologies in the Development phase ensures iterative progress and faster delivery of working prototypes.

4. Enhances Quality

- Each phase of the System Life Cycle includes checks and balances to ensure the system meets quality standards.
- **Example**: Testing and evaluation during the Development phase ensure that the AI model performs accurately and reliably.

5. Facilitates Collaboration

- The System Life Cycle encourages collaboration between stakeholders, including business teams, technical teams, and end-users.
- **Example**: In the Planning phase, business stakeholders provide input on requirements, while technical teams assess feasibility.

6. Ensures Scalability and Maintainability

- Systems developed using the System Life Cycle are designed with scalability and maintainability in mind, ensuring they can evolve with business needs.

- **Example**: An AI system for customer recommendations is built on a scalable cloud infrastructure, allowing it to handle increasing data volumes over time.

7. Provides a Framework for Continuous Improvement

- The System Life Cycle includes phases for monitoring, maintenance, and optimization, ensuring systems remain effective over time.

- **Example**: After deployment, an AI system is continuously monitored and updated to improve accuracy and adapt to changing business needs.

HOW THE SYSTEM LIFE CYCLE APPLIES TO AI SYSTEMS

Below is a detailed explanation of how the **System Life Cycle** applies to AI systems, mapped to the **AI System Lifecycle** (Planning, Design, Development, Implementation):

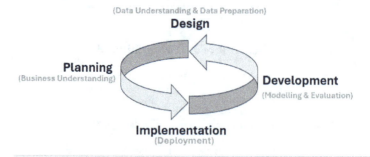

1. PLANNING (BUSINESS UNDERSTANDING)

- **Objective**: Define the problem, set goals, and align AI initiatives with business needs.

- **Activities**:

  - o Identify business problems and opportunities.

  - o Define success metrics (e.g., ROI, accuracy).

  - o Assess feasibility and resource requirements.

- **Example**: A bank plans to use AI to detect fraudulent transactions, aiming to reduce fraud losses by 20%.

2. DESIGN (DATA UNDERSTANDING & PREPARATION)

- **Objective**: Understand and prepare the data needed for AI modeling.

- **Activities**:

  - o Collect and analyze data from relevant sources.

  - o Clean, preprocess, and transform data.

  - o Design the AI solution architecture.

- **Example**: A retail company prepares customer data

(e.g., purchase history, browsing behavior) to build a recommendation engine.

3. DEVELOPMENT (MODELING & EVALUATION)

- **Objective**: Build, train, and evaluate AI models.
- **Activities**:
  - o Select appropriate algorithms and frameworks.
  - o Train models using prepared data.
  - o Evaluate model performance and refine as needed.
- **Example**: A healthcare provider trains a diagnostic AI model on patient data and evaluates its accuracy using test datasets.

4. IMPLEMENTATION (DEPLOYMENT)

- **Objective**: Deploy the AI system and integrate it into business processes.
- **Activities**:
  - o Deploy the AI model into production.
  - o Integrate with existing systems and workflows.
  - o Monitor performance and gather user feedback.
- **Example**: An e-commerce platform deploys an AI-powered chatbot to handle customer inquiries.

5. MONITORING AND MAINTENANCE

- **Objective**: Ensure the AI system remains effective and

adapts to changing needs.

- **Activities**:
    - o Continuously monitor system performance.
    - o Update models with new data.
    - o Address issues and optimize the system.
- **Example**: A logistics company monitors an AI system for route optimization and updates it with real-time traffic data.

Planning	Design	Development	Implementation
(Business Understanding)	(Data Understanding & Data Preparation)	(Modelling & Evaluation)	(Deployment)

AI SYSTEM LIFECYCLE WITH GOVERNANCE CONTROLS

1. PLANNING (BUSINESS UNDERSTANDING)

Governance Focus: *Risk Classification & Legal Compliance*

Key Activities:

- **Define use case** and classify AI system under regulations:
    - o **EU AI Act:** Is it *prohibited/high-risk/limited-risk* (Art. 5/6)?
    - o **Sector-specific laws:** HIPAA (healthcare), FCRA (hiring).

- Conduct **Algorithmic Impact Assessment (AIA)**.
- Assign roles: **Data Protection Officer (DPO), AI Ethics Board**.

Governance Outputs:

✅ *Regulatory   Classification   Report*

✅ *Stakeholder Sign-off* (Legal, Security, Business)

Example:

A bank's loan-approval AI is classified as **high-risk** *under EU AI Act Annex III. Requires conformity assessment (Art. 43).*

2. DESIGN (DATA UNDERSTANDING & PREPARATION)

Governance Focus: *Bias Mitigation & Privacy-by-Design*

Key Activities:

- **Data provenance tracking** (EU AI Act Art. 10).
- **Bias audits** using tools (e.g., **Aequitas, Fairness Indicators**).
- Anonymize data (**GDPR**), implement **role-based access controls**.

Governance Outputs:

✅ *Bias Audit Report*

✅ *Data Protection Impact Assessment (DPIA)*

Example:

*A facial recognition system excludes underrepresented demographics →
redesign dataset per* **ISO/IEC 24027**.

3. DEVELOPMENT (MODELING & EVALUATION)

Governance Focus: *Transparency & Security*

Key Activities:

- Document model architecture (**EU AI Act Art. 11**).
- Test for:
    - ○ **Robustness** (adversarial attacks via **CleverHans**).
    - ○ **Explainability** (SHAP values, LIME).
- **Third-party validation** for high-risk AI (e.g., **TÜV SÜD**).

Governance Outputs:

✅ *Model Card* (Metrics, limitations)

✅ *Conformity Assessment* (EU AI Act Art. 43)

Example:

A hiring tool fails **disparate impact analysis** → *recalibrate decision thresholds.*

4. IMPLEMENTATION (DEPLOYMENT)

Governance Focus: *Human Oversight & Continuous Monitoring*

Key Activities:

- Deploy with **human-in-the-loop** (EU AI Act Art. 14).
- Set up real-time monitoring for:
    - ○ **Performance drift** (e.g., **Evidently AI**).
    - ○ **Anomalies** (e.g., sudden bias spikes).
- **Incident response plan** (report breaches per EU AI Act Art. 62).

Governance Outputs:

✅ *Monitoring Dashboard*

✅ *Audit Trail* (All model changes)

Example:

A chatbot starts generating harmful content → rollback + incident report to EU database.

KEY GOVERNANCE TOOLS

Phase	*Tool*	*Purpose*
Planning	**NIST AI RMF**	Risk categorization
Design	**IBM Fairness 360**	Bias detection
Development	**TensorFlow Privacy**	Differential privacy
Implementation	**MLflow**	Model versioning & audit logs

AI Leadership & Governance

The rapid advancement of Artificial Intelligence (AI) is not only transforming industries but also fundamentally altering the landscape of leadership. Leaders today face unprecedented challenges and opportunities in navigating the complexities of AI adoption and integration. This chapter delves into the essential leadership traits, required transformations, and the evolving role of leaders in the AI-driven world.

AI leadership is the ability to guide an organization in leveraging artificial intelligence (AI) to achieve strategic goals, drive innovation, and create value. It involves not only understanding the technical aspects of AI but also fostering a culture of innovation, ensuring ethical practices, and aligning AI initiatives with business objectives. In the era of digital transformation, AI leadership is critical for organizations to stay competitive, adapt to change, and harness the full potential of AI technologies.

WHAT IS AI LEADERSHIP?

AI leadership encompasses the following key dimensions:

1. Vision and Strategy:
    o Defining a clear vision for how AI will transform the organization.
    o Developing a strategic roadmap for AI adoption and integration.

2. Technical Understanding:
    o Understanding the capabilities and limitations of AI technologies.
    o Staying informed about advancements in AI, machine learning, and data science.

3. Change Management:
    o Driving cultural change to embrace AI and data-driven decision-making.
    o Overcoming resistance to AI adoption within the organization.

4. Ethical and Responsible AI:
    o Ensuring AI systems are fair, transparent, and accountable.

o   Addressing ethical concerns such as bias, privacy, and security.

5. Collaboration and Communication:

    o   Bridging the gap between technical teams and business stakeholders.

    o   Communicating the value of AI to employees, customers, and investors.

6. Talent Development:

    o   Building and nurturing AI talent within the organization.

    o   Upskilling employees to work effectively with AI technologies.

7. Innovation and Experimentation:

    o   Encouraging a culture of experimentation and risk-taking.

    o   Supporting pilot projects and scaling successful AI initiatives.

WHY DO ORGANIZATIONS NEED AI LEADERSHIP?

The rapid adoption of AI technologies has created a pressing need for AI leadership. Here's why organizations need strong AI leaders:

1. Navigating Complexity

- AI projects are complex and require a deep understanding of both technology and business.
- AI leaders can simplify this complexity and guide

organizations in making informed decisions.

2. Aligning AI with Business Goals

- Without proper leadership, AI initiatives may fail to deliver value or align with organizational objectives.
- AI leaders ensure that AI projects support the company's strategic priorities.

3. Driving Cultural Change

- AI adoption often requires a shift in mindset and culture.
- AI leaders can inspire and motivate employees to embrace AI and data-driven decision-making.

4. Ensuring Ethical AI Practices

- AI systems can have unintended consequences, such as bias or privacy violations.
- AI leaders prioritize ethical considerations and ensure responsible AI practices.

5. Building AI Capabilities

- Organizations need skilled talent to develop, deploy, and manage AI solutions.
- AI leaders focus on talent development and creating a pipeline of AI expertise.

6. Staying Competitive

- AI is a key driver of innovation and competitive advantage.
- AI leaders help organizations stay ahead of the curve by leveraging AI effectively.

7. Managing Risks

- AI projects come with risks, such as technical failures or regulatory non-compliance.

- AI leaders implement governance frameworks to mitigate these risks.

KEY RESPONSIBILITIES OF AI LEADERS

AI leaders play a critical role in shaping the future of their organizations. Their responsibilities include:

1. Defining the AI Vision:
   o Articulate a clear vision for how AI will transform the organization.
   o Communicate this vision to stakeholders at all levels.

2. Developing an AI Strategy:
   o Create a roadmap for AI adoption, including short-term and long-term goals.
   o Prioritize AI use cases based on business value and feasibility.

3. Building AI Capabilities:
   o Invest in AI talent, tools, and infrastructure.
   o Partner with external experts and technology providers.

4. Fostering a Culture of Innovation:
   o Encourage experimentation and risk-taking.

o   Celebrate successes and learn from failures.

5. Ensuring Ethical AI:

    o   Establish guidelines for ethical AI development and deployment.

    o   Conduct regular audits to ensure compliance.

6. Driving Collaboration:

    o   Break down silos and foster collaboration between technical and business teams.

    o   Create cross-functional teams to work on AI projects.

7. Measuring Success:

    o   Define KPIs to track the impact of AI initiatives.

    o   Use data-driven insights to refine strategies and improve outcomes.

QUALITIES OF EFFECTIVE AI LEADERS

Effective AI leaders possess a unique combination of technical knowledge, business acumen, and leadership skills. Key qualities include:

1. Strategic Thinking:

    o   Ability to align AI initiatives with business goals.

    o   Visionary mindset to anticipate future trends and opportunities.

2. Technical Literacy:

    o   Understanding of AI technologies, data science,

and machine learning.

- o Ability to communicate technical concepts to non-technical stakeholders.

3. Emotional Intelligence:
   - o Empathy and ability to inspire and motivate teams.
   - o Skill in managing resistance to change.

4. Ethical Mindset:
   - o Commitment to fairness, transparency, and accountability in AI.
   - o Awareness of the societal impact of AI technologies.

5. Adaptability:
   - o Willingness to experiment and learn from failures.
   - o Ability to pivot strategies based on feedback and changing circumstances.
   - o

"The most dangerous leadership myth is that leaders are born. AI leadership is a mindset forged through curiosity, courage, and systems thinking."
—Adapted from Warren Bennis

Why This Matters

In 2023, a Fortune 500 company scrapped a $12M AI project after its biased loan algorithm sparked regulatory scrutiny. The root cause? Not flawed code, but flawed leadership.

THE THREE PILLARS OF THE AI LEADER'S MINDSET

1. Technical Fluency

"Speak AI, but don't need to code it."

What It Is:

- Understanding core AI concepts (e.g., how LLMs generate text, what "overfitting" means) without hands-on coding.
- Translating technical risks into business terms (e.g., *"Our model's 5% bias rate could trigger EU fines"*)

Why It Matters:

- **Case Study:** When *Airbnb's pricing algorithm* was accused of discrimination, CEO Brian Chesky ordered an overhaul because he grasped the technical implications.

How to Develop It:

- Take *CS50's Introduction to AI* (Harvard's free course).
- Host monthly "AI 101" sessions where engineers explain one model in plain language.

Leadership Litmus Test:

Can you explain to your board how your AI system makes decisions in 3 minutes?

2. ETHICAL COURAGE

"Willing to press pause."

What It Is:

- Halting deployments over ethical concerns (bias, privacy, misinformation), even under revenue pressure.
- Creating psychological safety for teams to voice concerns.

Why It Matters:

- **Failure Case:** *Zillow's AI-powered home-flipping disaster* ($500M loss) could've been avoided if leaders questioned the model's volatility assumptions.

How to Operationalize It:

- Implement an *AI Ethics Review Board* with veto power (like Microsoft's AETHER committee).
- Use *red teaming.* Pay external experts to stress-test your AI for harm.

Leadership   Litmus   Test:

Would you delay your flagship AI product 6 months to fix a bias issue?

3. SYSTEMS THINKING

"Seeing beyond the algorithm."

What It Is:

- Anticipating second-order effects (e.g., *"If our hiring AI favors Ivy League candidates, it could homogenize our workforce"*).

- Mapping stakeholders: regulators, employees, marginalized communities.

Why It Matters:

- **Success Case:** *Rwanda's drone delivery AI* succeeded because leaders considered infrastructure (charging stations), not just the tech.

How to Cultivate It:

- Conduct *pre-mortems*: *"Imagine our AI failed catastrophically—what likely caused it?"*

- Use *stakeholder impact maps* (see template below).

Leadership   Litmus   Test:

Can you name 3 unintended consequences your AI might trigger in 5 years?

TOOLS FOR THE AI LEADER'S MINDSET

---

1. STAKEHOLDER IMPACT MAP

Stakehol	Potential	Mitigation Plan

der	Harm	
Employ ees	Job displacement fears	Reskilling programs + transparency
Regulat ors	Non-compliance fines	Pre-emptive EU AI Act audit

2. AI DECISION JOURNAL

Example Entry:

- **Date:** March 15, 2024
- **Decision:** Approved beta launch of customer service chatbot.
- **Ethical Check:** Bias audit showed 8% error rate for non-native English speakers → added human fallback option.

CASE STUDY: MICROSOFT'S RESPONSIBLE AI JOURNEY

Challenge: In 2016, Microsoft's Tay chatbot became racist within 24 hours.

Leadership Response:

1. **Technical Fluency:** Satya Nadella demanded explainability tools for future models.
2. **Ethical Courage:** Established AI ethics review gates before deployments.
3. **Systems Thinking:** Partnered with NGOs to assess

societal risks of Azure AI tools.

Result: Avoided repeat scandals while growing AI revenue to $30B/year.

1. Invest in Training:
   o Provide leadership training programs focused on AI and digital transformation.
   o Encourage leaders to stay updated on AI trends and technologies.

2. Hire AI-Savvy Leaders:
   o Recruit leaders with a strong background in AI, data science, or technology.
   o Look for candidates with a track record of driving innovation.

3. Create AI Leadership Roles:
   o Establish roles like Chief AI Officer (CAIO) or AI Strategy Lead.
   o Empower these leaders to drive AI initiatives across the organization.

4. Foster a Culture of Learning:
   o Encourage leaders to experiment with AI and learn from failures.
   o Provide resources for continuous learning and development.

5. Promote Ethical AI Practices:
   o Train leaders on the ethical implications of AI.

o   Establish governance frameworks to ensure responsible AI use.

AI leadership is no longer optional—it's a necessity for organizations looking to thrive in the age of AI. Effective AI leaders combine technical expertise, strategic thinking, and ethical awareness to guide their organizations through the complexities of AI adoption. By investing in AI leadership, organizations can unlock the full potential of AI, drive innovation, and create lasting value.

Crisis Leadership in AI: A Step-by-Step Playbook for Failures

---

When AI systems fail—whether due to bias, security breaches, or unintended harm—the response can define an organization's reputation, legal liability, and future trust. Below is a **detailed, actionable playbook** for AI leaders to navigate crises effectively.

Step 1: Pause the System
Why?
- Continuing operations can amplify harm (e.g., biased hiring tools rejecting qualified candidates).
- Regulatory penalties (e.g., EU AI Act fines) worsen if

harm persists.

How?

- **Immediate Actions:**
    - o **Technical:** Disable API endpoints, roll back model versions.
    - o **Operational:** Notify customer support teams to halt AI-dependent processes.
- **Example:**
    - o *Twitter's image-cropping AI* was paused after bias toward lighter-skinned faces was exposed.

Step 2: Diagnose the Root Cause

Key Questions to Ask:

1. **Data Issue?**
    - o Was training data skewed? (e.g., *Amazon's hiring tool trained on male-dominated resumes.*)
2. **Model Issue?**
    - o Did the algorithm amplify biases? (e.g., *COMPAS recidivism algorithm's racial bias.*)
3. **Deployment Issue?**
    - o Was monitoring inadequate? (e.g., *Microsoft's Tay chatbot exploited by users.*)

Tools for Diagnosis:

- **Bias Detection:** IBM Fairness 360, Aequitas
- **Security Forensics:** Adversarial Robustness Toolbox
- **Data Lineage:** MLflow, Databricks Delta Lake

Step 3: Disclose Transparently

Why?

- Required under **EU AI Act (Art. 62)** for high-risk AI incidents.
- Builds trust—cover-ups backfire (e.g., *Uber's 2016 data breach concealment*).

How?

1. **Internal Communication:**
   - Inform employees with a **blameless post-mortem** (focus on systems, not people).

2. **External Communication:**
   - **Public Statement:** Acknowledge the issue, explain steps being taken (see template below).
   - **Regulatory Reporting:** Submit to EU database (if applicable).

Example Disclosure Statement:

"We've paused our [AI system] after identifying [issue]. We're working with [independent auditor] to rectify this and will share updates by [date]."

Step 4: Fix with External Audits

Why?

- Self-investigations lack credibility.
- External audits are often mandated (e.g., EU AI Act's conformity assessments).

How?

1. **Engage Third Parties:**
   o **Bias Audits:** Hire firms like O'Neil Risk Consulting.
   o **Security Audits:** Use NCC Group or Trail of Bits.
2. **Remediation Plan:**
   o Retrain models with debiased data.
   o Implement **human-in-the-loop** safeguards.

Case Study:

- *Facebook (Meta) used external auditors* after its ad-targeting AI was found discriminatory.

Real-World AI Crisis Playbook

SCENARIO: A HEALTHCARE AI MISDIAGNOSES 10% OF DIABETIC PATIENTS.

1. **Pause:** Disable the AI in hospitals.
2. **Diagnose:** Found training data lacked diverse age groups.
3. **Disclose:** Notified regulators and hospitals within 24 hours.
4. **Fix:** Partnered with Mayo Clinic to retrain the model.

Proactive Crisis Prevention

1. Pre-Crisis Prep

- **Incident Response Team:** Designate an **AI Crisis Lead** (legal + tech + PR).
- **Run Drills:** Simulate AI failures (e.g., "What if our chatbot leaks data?").

2. Monitoring Triggers

Risk	Early Warning Sign	Action
Bias	Disparate impact ratio >1.25	Audit model + pause if confirmed.
Security	Unusual inference requests	Investigate for adversarial attacks.

Leadership Litmus Test

"If your AI caused harm today, does your team know:

1. *Who can pause it?*
2. *Who investigates?*
3. *Who speaks to the press?"*

If not, revisit this playbook immediately.

KEY CHANGES LEADERS MUST MAKE
MINDSET SHIFT:

- **From "AI is a threat"** → **To "AI is an enabler"**
- **From "AI replaces people"** → **To "AI augments people"**
- **From "Experience-based decisions"** → **To "AI +**

experience = smarter decisions"

- From "One-time learning" → To "Lifelong learning"

AI WON'T REPLACE LEADERS—BUT LEADERS WHO DON'T ADAPT WILL BE LEFT BEHIND!

"Rate Your AI Leadership Traits (1-5)"
Self-Assessment

Instructions: Score each trait from 1 (Weak) to 5 (Strong) based on your current behaviors. Use the results to identify development areas.

1. Technical Fluency

"I understand AI's capabilities/limits without needing to code."

- 5: I explain ML concepts (e.g., overfitting, LLMs) to non-tech stakeholders.

- 3: I grasp basics but rely heavily on experts for details.

- 1: I avoid technical discussions.

  Example: *Satya Nadella discussing transformer models in interviews.*

2. Ethical Courage

"I challenge unethical AI use, even under pressure."

- 5: I halted a project due to bias/privacy concerns (e.g., IBM's facial recognition exit).
- 3: I raise concerns but defer to leadership.
- 1: I prioritize speed over ethics.

  Example: *Timnit Gebru's stance on bias in AI.*

3. Strategic Agility

"I pivot AI strategy based on new risks/opportunities."

- 5: I revised our roadmap after ChatGPT's release to stay competitive.
- 3: I react to changes but lack proactive planning.
- 1: I stick to original plans rigidly.

  Example: *NVIDIA's shift from gaming to AI chips.*

4. Cross-Disciplinary Collaboration

"I bridge gaps between tech, legal, and business teams."

- 5: I lead mixed teams (engineers + lawyers + designers) weekly.
- 3: I involve other departments occasionally.
- 1: I work in silos.

  Example: *DeepMind's AlphaFold team including biologists.*

5. Risk Intelligence

"I quantify and mitigate AI risks (bias, security, compliance)."

- 5: I use frameworks like NIST AI RMF and EU AI Act checklists.
- 3: I address risks ad hoc.
- 1: I assume "the engineers will handle it."

  Example: *EU's Margrethe Vestager regulating AI proactively.*

6. Transparency Advocacy

"I demand explainability and document AI decisions openly."

- 5: I publish model cards/audit reports (e.g., IBM's AI FactSheets).
- 3: I share limited details with internal teams.
- 1: I treat AI as a "black box."

  Example: *Google's Responsible AI practices.*

7. Talent Catalyst

"I attract/retain AI talent through purpose and growth."

- 5: I sponsor upskilling programs and mission-driven projects.
- 3: I rely on HR to manage talent.
- 1: I see AI talent as replaceable.

  Example: *OpenAI's research culture.*

8. Stakeholder Alignment

"I secure buy-in from execs, employees, and regulators."

- 5: I map stakeholder concerns (e.g., job loss fears) and address them.
- 3: I communicate updates but don't tailor messaging.
- 1: I avoid engaging skeptics.

  Example: *Rwanda's health drone AI public-private partnership.*

9. Long-Term Vision

"I balance quick wins with responsible moonshots."

- 5: I allocate 20%+ budget to long-term AI safety research.

- 3: I focus on 1–2 year ROI.

- 1: I chase hype cycles.

  Example: *Elon Musk's OpenAI founding vision (before divergence).*

10. Humility & Learning Mindset

"I admit mistakes and learn from failures."

- 5: I conduct blameless post-mortems (e.g., Google's Bard launch review).

- 3: I acknowledge errors privately.

- 1: I deflect criticism.

  Example: *Sundar Pichai admitting Bard's flaws post-launch.*

Scoring Guide

- *45–50: Visionary AI Leader (e.g., Nadella, Gebru)*

- *35–44: Growing Leader (focus on 1–2 weak traits)*

- *25–34: Risky Gap (prioritize ethics/strategy)*

- *<25: Red Flag (seek mentorship/training immediately)*

ACTIONABLE NEXT STEPS

1. **For Low Scores (1–2):**

   o *Ethics:* **Complete MIT's** *Ethics of AI* **course (free).**

   o *Technical Fluency:* **Take** *AI for Everyone* **(Coursera).**

2. **For Medium Scores (3–4):**

    ○ Join *Partnership on AI* for peer learning.

    ○ Shadow cross-functional teams for 1 month.

3. **For High Scores (5):**

    ○ Mentor others using this assessment.

    ○ Publish a case study on your leadership approach.

EXAMPLE ASSESSMENT

Trait	Score
Technical Fluency	4
Ethical Courage	5
Strategic Agility	3
Total	38/50

Responsible AI Act

Responsible AI and **Trustworthy AI** are critical concepts in the development and deployment of AI systems. They ensure that AI technologies are ethical, fair, transparent, and aligned with human values. Below is a detailed explanation of **Trustworthy AI**, its principles, and how organizations can implement it.

TRUSTWORTHY AI: PRINCIPLES AND PRACTICES

Trustworthy AI refers to AI systems that are designed and deployed in a way that is **ethical, transparent, fair, and accountable**. It ensures that AI technologies are aligned with human values and societal norms, building trust among users and

80

stakeholders.

KEY PRINCIPLES OF TRUSTWORTHY AI

Trustworthy AI is built on several core principles that guide its development and deployment:

a. Fairness:

- AI systems should treat all individuals and groups fairly, without bias or discrimination.
- **Example**: Ensuring that a hiring algorithm does not favor one gender or ethnicity over another.

b. Transparency:

- AI systems should be transparent in their decision-making processes, allowing users to understand how decisions are made.
- **Example**: Providing explanations for why a loan application was rejected by an AI system.

c. Accountability:

- Organizations and individuals responsible for AI systems should be accountable for their actions and decisions.
- **Example**: Establishing clear roles and responsibilities for AI development and deployment.

d. Privacy:

- AI systems should respect user privacy and protect personal data.
- **Example**: Implementing data encryption and access controls to protect sensitive information.

e. Security:

- AI systems should be secure and resilient against attacks and misuse.

- **Example**: Using robust cybersecurity measures to protect AI models and data.

f. Robustness:

- AI systems should perform reliably and consistently under different conditions.

- **Example**: Ensuring that a self-driving car can operate safely in various weather conditions.

g. Inclusivity:

- AI systems should be designed to benefit all individuals and communities, including marginalized groups.

- **Example**: Developing AI-powered healthcare solutions that are accessible to people with disabilities.

PRACTICES FOR BUILDING TRUSTWORTHY AI

To implement Trustworthy AI, organizations should adopt the following practices:

a. Bias Mitigation:

- Identify and mitigate biases in data and algorithms to ensure fairness.

- **Example**: Conducting bias audits and using diverse datasets for training AI models.

b. Explainability:

- Develop AI systems that can explain their decisions in a

way that is understandable to users.

- **Example**: Using techniques like LIME (Local Interpretable Model-agnostic Explanations) to explain model predictions.

c. Ethical Guidelines:

- Establish ethical guidelines and principles for AI development and deployment.
- **Example**: Creating an AI ethics board to oversee AI projects and ensure compliance with ethical standards.

d. Data Governance:

- Implement robust data governance practices to ensure data quality, security, and privacy.
- **Example**: Using data anonymization techniques to protect user privacy.

e. Continuous Monitoring:

- Continuously monitor AI systems to ensure they perform as intended and address any issues that arise.
- **Example**: Setting up real-time monitoring tools to track the performance of an AI-powered chatbot.

f. Stakeholder Engagement:

- Engage with stakeholders, including users, employees, and communities, to understand their needs and concerns.
- **Example**: Conducting surveys and focus groups to gather feedback on AI systems.

g. Regulatory Compliance:

- Ensure that AI systems comply with relevant laws and regulations.
- **Example**: Adhering to GDPR requirements for data protection and privacy.

Several frameworks and guidelines have been developed to help organizations implement Trustworthy AI:

a. EU Ethics Guidelines for Trustworthy AI:

- Developed by the European Commission, these guidelines provide a framework for ethical AI development.
- **Key Principles**: Human agency, technical robustness, privacy, transparency, and accountability.

b. IEEE Ethically Aligned Design:

- A framework developed by IEEE to ensure that AI systems are aligned with ethical principles.
- **Key Principles**: Human rights, well-being, accountability, and transparency.

c. AI Fairness 360 (AIF360):

- An open-source toolkit developed by IBM to detect and mitigate bias in AI models.
- **Key Features**: Algorithms and metrics for fairness assessment and mitigation.

d. Google's AI Principles:

- Google's guidelines for ethical AI development, focusing on social benefit, fairness, and accountability.

- **Key Principles**: Avoid creating or reinforcing unfair bias, be accountable to people, and uphold high standards of scientific excellence.

e. Microsoft's Responsible AI Principles:

- Microsoft's framework for responsible AI development, emphasizing fairness, reliability, and inclusivity.

- **Key Principles**: Fairness, reliability and safety, privacy and security, inclusiveness, transparency, and accountability.

CHALLENGES IN IMPLEMENTING TRUSTWORTHY AI

While the principles of Trustworthy AI are clear, implementing them can be challenging:

a. Bias in Data and Algorithms:

- AI systems can inherit biases from training data, leading to unfair outcomes.

- **Solution**: Use diverse datasets and conduct bias audits.

b. Lack of Transparency:

- Complex AI models, such as deep neural networks, can be difficult to interpret.

- **Solution**: Develop explainable AI techniques and provide clear documentation.

c. Regulatory Complexity:

- Navigating the complex landscape of AI regulations can be challenging.

- **Solution**: Stay informed about relevant laws and work with legal experts.

d. Resource Constraints:

- Implementing Trustworthy AI practices can require significant resources.

- **Solution**: Prioritize key areas and leverage open-source tools.

e. Ethical Dilemmas:

- AI systems may face ethical dilemmas, such as prioritizing one life over another in autonomous vehicles.

- **Solution**: Establish ethical guidelines and involve diverse stakeholders in decision-making.

REAL-WORLD EXAMPLES OF TRUSTWORTHY AI

IBM Watson for Oncology:

- IBM's AI system assists doctors in diagnosing and treating cancer.

- **Trustworthy AI Practices**: Ensures transparency by providing explanations for treatment recommendations and adheres to strict data privacy standards.

Google's AI for Social Good:

- Google uses AI to address global challenges, such as predicting floods and protecting wildlife.

- **Trustworthy AI Practices**: Focuses on fairness, inclusivity, and social benefit.

Microsoft's AI for Accessibility:

- Microsoft develops AI tools to empower people with disabilities.

- **Trustworthy AI Practices**: Ensures inclusivity and accessibility in AI design.

Trustworthy AI is essential for ensuring that AI systems are ethical, fair, transparent, and aligned with human values. By adhering to principles like fairness, transparency, and accountability, and implementing practices such as bias mitigation and continuous monitoring, organizations can build AI systems that are trusted by users and stakeholders. Frameworks like the EU Ethics Guidelines and tools like AI Fairness 360 provide valuable guidance for achieving Trustworthy AI.

Below is a detailed explanation of the **EU AI Act, ISO 42001, OECD AI Principles, Fair Information Principles (FIPs)**, and **UNESCO's Recommendation on the Ethics of Artificial Intelligence**. These frameworks and guidelines provide a comprehensive approach to ensuring ethical, fair, and responsible AI development and deployment.

EU AI Act

The **EU AI Act** is a proposed regulation by the European Union to ensure that AI systems are safe, transparent, and aligned with EU values. It is one of the first comprehensive legal frameworks for AI.

Key Provisions:

1. **Risk-Based Approach:**
   - AI systems are categorized into four risk levels: **unacceptable risk, high risk, limited risk,** and **minimal risk.**
   - **Unacceptable Risk:** AI systems that pose a clear threat to safety, livelihoods, and rights are banned (e.g., social scoring by governments).
   - **High Risk:** AI systems in critical areas like healthcare, transportation, and law enforcement are subject to strict requirements (e.g., transparency, data governance).
   - **Limited Risk:** AI systems with minimal risk (e.g., chatbots) require transparency (e.g., informing users they are interacting with AI).
   - **Minimal Risk:** AI systems with no significant risk (e.g., AI-powered video games) are largely unregulated.

2. **Transparency and Explainability:**
   - High-risk AI systems must provide clear information about their functioning and decision-making processes.
   - Example: An AI system used in hiring must explain why a candidate was rejected.

3. **Data Governance:**
   - High-risk AI systems must use high-quality

datasets to minimize biases and errors.

- o Example: A healthcare AI system must use diverse and representative patient data.

4. **Human Oversight:**

- o High-risk AI systems must include human oversight to ensure accountability.
- o Example: A self-driving car must allow human intervention in critical situations.

5. **Compliance and Enforcement:**

- o Organizations must conduct conformity assessments and maintain documentation for high-risk AI systems.
- o Example: A company using AI for credit scoring must demonstrate compliance with the EU AI Act.

ISO 42001 (AI MANAGEMENT SYSTEM STANDARD)

ISO 42001 is an upcoming international standard for AI management systems. It provides guidelines for organizations to manage AI systems responsibly and ethically.

Key Components:

1. **AI Governance:**

- o Establish policies and procedures for AI

development and deployment.

- o Example: Creating an AI ethics board to oversee AI projects.

2. **Risk Management**:
   - o Identify and mitigate risks associated with AI systems.
   - o Example: Conducting risk assessments for AI systems used in healthcare.

3. **Transparency and Explainability**:
   - o Ensure that AI systems are transparent and their decisions are explainable.
   - o Example: Providing documentation on how an AI model makes predictions.

4. **Data Quality and Privacy**:
   - o Ensure that data used for AI systems is accurate, complete, and privacy-compliant.
   - o Example: Implementing data anonymization techniques to protect user privacy.

5. **Continuous Improvement**:
   - o Monitor and improve AI systems over time.
   - o Example: Regularly updating an AI model with new data to improve accuracy.

OECD AI PRINCIPLES

The **OECD AI Principles** are a set of guidelines developed by the Organisation for Economic Co-operation and Development (OECD) to promote trustworthy AI.

Key Principles:

1. **Inclusive Growth, Sustainable Development, and Well-Being:**
   - AI should benefit people and the planet.
   - Example: Using AI to address climate change and improve healthcare.

2. **Human-Centered Values and Fairness:**
   - AI should respect human rights, diversity, and fairness.
   - Example: Ensuring that AI systems do not discriminate based on gender or ethnicity.

3. **Transparency and Explainability:**
   - AI systems should be transparent and their decisions should be explainable.
   - Example: Providing clear explanations for AI-driven decisions in hiring.

4. **Robustness, Security, and Safety:**
   - AI systems should be secure, reliable, and safe.
   - Example: Ensuring that autonomous vehicles operate safely in all conditions.

5. **Accountability:**
   - Organizations and individuals responsible for AI systems should be accountable.
   - Example: Establishing clear roles and

responsibilities for AI development and deployment.

FAIR INFORMATION PRINCIPLES (FIPs)

The **Fair Information Principles (FIPs)** are a set of guidelines for data privacy and protection. They form the foundation of many data protection laws, including GDPR.

Key Principles:

1. **Notice:**
   o Individuals should be informed about how their data is collected and used.
   o Example: Providing a privacy policy on a website.

2. **Choice:**
   o Individuals should have control over how their data is used.
   o Example: Allowing users to opt out of data collection.

3. **Access:**
   o Individuals should have access to their data and be able to correct inaccuracies.

o Example: Providing users with access to their personal data stored by a company.

4. **Security**:

o Data should be protected from unauthorized access and breaches.

o Example: Encrypting sensitive customer data.

5. **Accountability**:

o Organizations should be accountable for complying with data protection principles.

o Example: Conducting regular audits to ensure compliance with privacy laws.

UNESCO's Recommendation on the Ethics of Artificial Intelligence

---

UNESCO's **Recommendation on the Ethics of Artificial Intelligence** provides a global framework for ethical AI development and deployment.

Key Principles:

1. **Human Rights and Dignity**:

o AI should respect and promote human rights and dignity.

o Example: Ensuring that AI systems do not infringe on privacy or freedom of expression.

2. **Sustainability**:

- o AI should contribute to environmental sustainability.
- o Example: Using AI to optimize energy consumption in data centers.

3. **Inclusivity**:
   - o AI should be inclusive and benefit all individuals and communities.
   - o Example: Developing AI-powered healthcare solutions that are accessible to marginalized groups.

4. **Transparency and Explainability**:
   - o AI systems should be transparent and their decisions should be explainable.
   - o Example: Providing clear explanations for AI-driven decisions in hiring.

5. **Accountability and Responsibility**:
   - o Organizations and individuals responsible for AI systems should be accountable.
   - o Example: Establishing clear roles and responsibilities for AI development and deployment.

6. **Ethical Governance**:
   - o AI systems should be governed by ethical principles and regulations.
   - o Example: Creating an AI ethics board to oversee AI projects.

COMPARISON OF FRAMEWORKS

Framework	Focus	Key Principles
EU AI Act	Legal regulation of AI systems in the EU.	Risk-based approach, transparency, data governance, human oversight.
ISO 42001	Management system standard for AI.	AI governance, risk management, transparency, data quality, continuous improvement.
OECD AI Principles	Global guidelines for trustworthy AI.	Inclusive growth, human-centered values, transparency, robustness, accountability.
Fair Information Principles (FIPs)	Data privacy and protection.	Notice, choice, access, security, accountability.
UNESCO's Recommendation	Global ethical	Human rights, sustainability, inclusivity,

framework	for	transparency,
AI.		accountability.

These frameworks and guidelines—**EU AI Act, ISO 42001, OECD AI Principles,** Fair Information Principles **(FIPs)**, and **UNESCO's Recommendation on the Ethics of Artificial Intelligence**—provide a comprehensive approach to ensuring ethical, fair, and responsible AI development and deployment. By adhering to these principles, organizations can build AI systems that are trustworthy, transparent, and aligned with human values.

AI GOVERNANCE FRAMEWORK & REGULATIONS

Building Blocks of AI Governance

Building Blocks of AI Governance in the Age of AI-talization

INTRODUCTION: THE ERA OF AI-TALIZATION

AI-talization represents a **paradigm shift**—a fundamental reimagining of business models, operations, and value creation through artificial intelligence. Unlike traditional digital transformation, AI-talization requires **strategic governance** to ensure AI adoption is **ethical, sustainable, and aligned with long-term business and societal goals**.

To navigate this transformation, we introduce the **AAE Framework (Aware, Arise, Enlight)**, which provides a structured approach to AI strategy, technology, and implementation. Underpinning this framework is **AI Governance (AO Governance—Alignment and**

Oversight Governance), ensuring that AI systems
are **responsibly managed, auditable, and value-driven.**

THE AAE FRAMEWORK FOR AI-TALIZATION

1. Power of Strategy → Aware (Business Vision & AI Alignment)

AI-talization begins with **strategic clarity**. Organizations must define how AI integrates with their mission while mitigating risks.

Key Components:

- **AI Vision & Roadmap** – How AI supports business objectives (e.g., automation, personalization, decision intelligence).

- **Stakeholder Alignment** – Engaging leadership, employees, regulators, and customers in AI strategy.

- **Ethical & Regulatory Compliance** – Adhering to GDPR, EU AI Act, and industry-specific guidelines.

- **Risk Assessment** – Identifying biases, security vulnerabilities, and operational risks early.

AI Governance (AO) Role:

- Establishes **AI ethics boards** and governance policies.

- Ensures AI strategy aligns with **corporate governance and ESG principles.**

2. POWER OF TECHNOLOGY → ARISE (EVOLVING AI & DIGITAL FOUNDATION)

AI-talization demands a **future-proof digital infrastructure** that enables scalability, security, and adaptability.

Key Components:

- **Data Governance** – Ensuring high-quality, unbiased, and legally compliant training data.
- **Explainable AI (XAI)** – Making AI decisions interpretable for audits and compliance.
- **AI Model Lifecycle Management** – From development to deployment, monitoring, and updates.
- **Cybersecurity & Robustness** – Protecting AI from adversarial attacks and misuse.

AI Governance (AO) Role:

- Defines **technical standards** for AI development (e.g., fairness metrics, bias detection).
- Implements **AI auditing frameworks** (e.g., model drift detection, performance benchmarks).

3. POWER OF VALUE → ENLIGHT (IMPLEMENTATION & MEASURING IMPACT)

AI must deliver **tangible business and societal value** while maintaining trust.

Key Components:

- **Change Management & Workforce Upskilling** – Preparing employees for AI-driven workflows.
- **Performance Metrics** – Measuring ROI, efficiency

gains, and ethical impact (e.g., fairness, transparency).

- **Continuous Monitoring & Feedback Loops** – Adjusting AI models based on real-world performance.

- **Stakeholder Transparency** – Communicating AI benefits, limitations, and decision-making processes.

AI Governance (AO) Role:

- Tracks **AI accountability** through structured reporting.

- Ensures **regulatory compliance** and public trust in AI systems.AI Governance (AO Governance) – Alignment & Oversight

WHAT IS AO GOVERNANCE?

AO Governance (Alignment and Oversight Governance) is a **structured process** ensuring AI systems are:

✓ **Aligned** with business strategy, ethics, and regulations.

✓ **Oversighted** through continuous monitoring, auditing, and accountability.

AO GOVERNANCE FRAMEWORK

Component	Description
Strategic Alignment	Ensures AI initiatives support business goals and comply with ethical standards.
Operational Oversight	Monitors AI performance, security, and fairness in real-world deployment.
Value & Impact	Measures ROI, societal impact, and

Governance	regulatory adherence.

AO GOVERNANCE PROCESSES & STRUCTURES

1. **AI Ethics & Compliance Board**
   - o Role: Defines AI policies, reviews high-risk AI projects, ensures regulatory adherence.
   - o Members: Legal, ethics, data science, and business leaders.

2. **AI Risk Management Framework**
   - o Identifies risks (bias, security, legal) and mitigation strategies.
   - o Example: **Red-teaming AI models** to test vulnerabilities.

3. **AI Auditing & Transparency Protocols**
   - o Conducts **algorithmic impact assessments**.
   - o Maintains **audit logs** for AI decision-making.

4. **Stakeholder Engagement & Reporting**
   - o Provides **transparency reports** to regulators and customers.
   - o Gathers feedback from employees and end-users.

CONCLUSION: GOVERNING AI-TALIZATION
FOR SUSTAINABLE SUCCESS

AI-talization is not just about technology—it's about **responsible transformation**. The **AAE Framework (Aware, Arise, Enlight)** provides the roadmap, while **AO Governance** ensures **alignment, accountability, and long-term value creation**.

KEY TAKEAWAYS

- ✓ **Aware (Strategy):** Align AI with business vision, ethics, and compliance.
- ✓ **Arise (Technology):** Build a secure, scalable, and transparent AI infrastructure.
- ✓ **Enlight (Value):** Measure impact, adapt, and maintain stakeholder trust.

AI Maturity Model: Assessing Organizational Readiness for AI-talization

---

INTRODUCTION TO AI MATURITY

AI maturity refers to an organization's ability to effectively develop, deploy, and govern artificial intelligence solutions.

As businesses progress through AI-talization, understanding their maturity level helps identify gaps and prioritize investments in strategy, technology, and governance.

THE 5-STAGE AI MATURITY MODEL

1. Ad Hoc (Initial Stage)

Characteristics:

- No formal AI strategy or governance
- Experimental, one-off AI projects
- Limited technical infrastructure
- No dedicated AI team or budget

Governance Implications:

- High risk of unvetted AI implementations
- Potential compliance violations
- No measurement of AI ROI

2. Emerging (Awareness Stage)

Characteristics:

- Basic AI strategy aligned with business goals
- Initial data governance frameworks
- Pilot projects with measured outcomes
- Small cross-functional AI team

Governance Focus:

- Developing ethical AI principles
- Implementing basic model documentation
- Starting risk assessment processes

3. Operational (Arise Stage)

Characteristics:

- Standardized AI development processes
- Dedicated MLOps infrastructure
- Measured ROI from multiple deployments
- Organization-wide AI training programs

Governance Requirements:

- Formal model monitoring systems
- Bias detection and mitigation protocols
- Regular compliance audits
- Clear AI accountability frameworks

4. Systemic (Enlight Stage)

Characteristics:

- AI embedded in core business processes
- Enterprise-wide data governance
- Continuous learning and adaptation
- AI-driven innovation pipeline

Governance Sophistication:

- Automated model governance
- Integrated risk management
- Transparent AI decision-making
- Stakeholder impact assessments

5. Transformational (AI-talized)

Characteristics:

- AI-first organizational mindset
- Self-improving AI ecosystems
- Predictive governance capabilities

- AI as primary value driver

Governance Excellence:

- Real-time compliance monitoring
- Ethical AI by design
- Automated impact reporting
- AI governance integrated with corporate strategy

Assessing AI Maturity: Key Dimensions

1. **Strategy & Leadership**
   - AI vision alignment with business goals
   - Executive sponsorship and investment
   - Change management readiness

2. **Data Foundations**
   - Data quality and accessibility
   - Privacy and security measures
   - Metadata management

3. **Technology & Infrastructure**
   - MLOps capabilities
   - Model lifecycle management
   - Scalable computing resources

4. **Talent & Culture**
   - AI skills across workforce
   - Cross-functional collaboration
   - Innovation mindset

5. **Governance & Ethics**
   - Compliance frameworks
   - Risk management processes

o   Transparency mechanisms

AI Maturity Assessment Framework

Dimension	Level 1	Level 2	Level 3	Level 4	Level 5
Strategy	No strategy	Emerging strategy	Defined roadmap	Integrated strategy	AI-driven transformation
Data	Siloed, poor quality	Basic governance	Standardized pipelines	Enterprise governance	Predictive data ecosystems
Technology	Manual processes	Basic automation	MLOps implementation	AI factory	Self-optimizing systems
People	No AI skills	Some specialists	Cross-functional teams	AI literacy across org	Continuous upskilling

Governance	Ad hoc compliance	Basic controls	Formal frameworks	Proactive governance	Ethical by design

ROADMAP FOR ADVANCING AI MATURITY

1. **Conduct Current State Assessment**
   o Evaluate all dimensions against maturity model
   o Identify critical gaps and quick wins

2. **Develop 12-24 Month Plan**
   o Prioritize foundational capabilities
   o Align with business priorities
   o Budget for technology and talent

3. **Implement Governance Foundations**
   o Establish AI ethics principles
   o Create model documentation standards
   o Initiate risk assessment processes

4. **Build Organizational Capabilities**
   o Upskill workforce through training
   o Develop center of excellence
   o Foster cross-functional collaboration

5. **Measure and Iterate**
   o Track KPIs for each dimension
   o Conduct quarterly maturity reviews
   o Adapt roadmap based on results

Conclusion: The Path to AI-talization

AI maturity is not a destination but a continuous journey. Organizations that systematically progress through maturity levels while strengthening governance frameworks will be best positioned to reap the benefits of AI-talization while mitigating risks. The AAE Framework provides the structure for this evolution, with AO Governance ensuring responsible advancement at each stage.

Industry-Specific AI Maturity Benchmarks for Effective AI-talization

INTRODUCTION TO INDUSTRY-SPECIFIC AI MATURITY

Different industries face unique challenges and opportunities in AI adoption. These benchmarks help organizations compare their progress against sector leaders and identify tailored pathways for advancing AI maturity within their specific operational contexts.

1. Financial Services AI Maturity

Current Adoption Levels:

- **Front-runner Banks:** 78% have operational AI in fraud detection
- **Insurance Leaders:** 65% use AI for claims processing automation
- **Investment Firms:** 92% of top quant funds employ AI-driven trading

KEY MATURITY INDICATORS:

Capability	Beginner	Emerging	Advanced	Leader
Risk Modelling Accuracy	±25% error	±15% error	±8% error	±3% error
Fraud Detection Speed	24-48 hrs	6-12 hrs	<1 hr	Real-time
Customer Chatbot Resolution	30%	55%	75%	92%
Regulatory Compliance	Manual checks	Basic automation	Integrated monitoring	Predictive compliance

Governance Priority: Explainable AI for auditability

(XAI adoption: 42% in 2023 → projected 68% by 2025)

---

2. Healthcare AI Maturity Benchmarks

Current Adoption Levels:

- **Top Hospitals:** 61% use AI for medical imaging analysis
- **Pharma R&D:** AI reduces drug discovery timelines by 30-40%
- **Health Systems:** 47% have operational patient risk stratification

KEY MATURITY INDICATORS:

Capability	Beginner	Emerging	Advanced	Leader
Diagnostic Accuracy	70-75%	80-85%	90-93%	95-98%
Patient Data Utilization	15% structured data	40% structured	75% structured unstructured	90% with real-time updates
Clinical Trial Matching	Manual process	Basic filters	AI recommendations	Automated enrolment

HIPAA Compliance	Annual audits	Quarterly checks	Continuous monitoring	Predictive compliance

Governance Priority: Patient data privacy (De-identification tech adoption: 58% in 2023)

Manufacturing AI Maturity

Benchmarks

Current Adoption Levels:

- **Smart Factories:** 54% use predictive maintenance
- **Automotive Leaders:** 82% employ computer vision for QA
- **Supply Chain:** 68% of top firms use AI demand forecasting

KEY MATURITY INDICATORS:

Capability	Beginner	Emerging	Advanced	Leader

Defect Detection Rate	85%	92%	97%	99.5%
Predictive Maintenance Accuracy	70%	82%	90%	95%
Inventory Optimization	5-10% waste	3-5% waste	1-3% waste	<1% waste
Energy Efficiency Gains	5-8%	10-12%	15-18%	20-25%

Governance Priority: Operational safety (AI safety certification adoption: 39% in 2023)

4. Retail & E-commerce AI Maturity Benchmarks

Current Adoption Levels:

- **Top Retailers:** 89% use AI for personalized recommendations
- **Logistics Leaders:** 76% employ route optimization AI
- **Inventory Management:** 63% of majors use AI forecasting

KEY MATURITY INDICATORS:

Capability	*Beginner*	*Emerging*	*Advanced*	*Leader*
Recommendation	2-3%	5-7%	10-12%	15-18%

Conversion Demand Forecasting Accuracy	±25%	±15%	±8%	±3%
Dynamic Pricing Effectiveness	3-5% lift	8-10% lift	12-15% lift	18-22% lift
Customer Service Automation	20% resolution	45%	70%	90%

Governance Priority: Algorithmic fairness (Bias testing adoption: 31% in 2023 → 53% projected 2025)

Cross-Industry Maturity Comparison

Industry	Avg. Maturity Score (2023)	Key Adoption Driver	Main Governance Challenge
Financial Services	3.4/5	Regulatory compliance	Explainability requirements
Healthcare	2.9/5	Diagnostic accuracy	Patient privacy
Manufacturing	3.1/5	Operational efficiency	Safety certifications
Retail	3.6/5	Customer experience	Algorithmic bias

Energy	2.7/5	Predictive maintenance	Infrastructure security

Actionable Recommendations by Industry

1. **Financial Services:**
   - o Implement real-time transaction monitoring (adoption gap: 32%)
   - o Develop model cards for all credit scoring AI (current: 28% compliance)

2. **Healthcare:**
   - o Adopt federated learning for multi-hospital collaborations (current: 19%)
   - o Implement AI explainability reports for clinicians (adoption: 41%)

3. **Manufacturing:**
   - o Deploy edge AI for real-time quality control (adoption gap: 44%)
   - o Establish AI safety review boards (current: 33% penetration)

4. **Retail:**
   - o Implement continuous bias testing for recommendations (current: 27%)

- Develop ethical personalization frameworks (adoption: 38%)

5. **Energy:**
   - Build digital twins for infrastructure monitoring (current: 29%)
   - Implement AI cybersecurity protocols (adoption gap: 41%)

Data Governance for AI

Why Data is the Lifeblood of AI: The Foundation of Intelligent Systems

Data is to AI what fuel is to an engine—without high-quality, relevant data, even the most sophisticated AI models cannot function effectively. Here's why data is absolutely critical for AI:

---

1. Data is the Core Ingredient of AI

AI systems learn patterns, make decisions, and improve performance based on data.

- **Training Data** → Teaches AI models how to recognize patterns (e.g., images, text, transactions).

- **Validation Data** → Ensures models generalize well to new, unseen inputs.

- **Real-World Data** → Keeps models updated and accurate over time.

Example:

- A facial recognition AI trained on diverse facial data performs better across different demographics.

- Poor or biased data leads to flawed AI (e.g., Amazon's biased hiring algorithm).

2. DATA QUALITY DIRECTLY IMPACTS AI PERFORMANCE

"Garbage In, Garbage Out" (GIGO) – If input data is flawed, AI outputs will be unreliable.

Data Issue	AI Impact
Incomplete Data	Models miss key patterns, leading to poor predictions
Biased Data	AI perpetuates discrimination (e.g., loan approval biases)
Noisy Data	AI learns incorrect correlations (e.g., misdiagnosing diseases)
Outdated Data	Models fail in real-world scenarios (e.g., stock market crashes)

Example:

- A healthcare AI trained on mostly male patient data may misdiagnose conditions in women.

3. Data Determines AI's Ethical & Fair Behavior

- **Bias in Data** → **Bias in AI** (e.g., racial/gender discrimination in hiring tools).
- **Transparency & Explainability** depend on well-documented data sources.
- **Regulatory Compliance** (GDPR, EU AI Act) requires auditable, fair data practices.

Example:

- **Facial recognition AI** trained mostly on lighter-skinned faces performs poorly on darker skin tones.

4. Data Fuels Continuous AI Improvement

- **Feedback Loops:** Real-world data helps AI adapt (e.g., recommendation systems like Netflix).
- **Retraining:** Models decay over time without fresh data (e.g., ChatGPT's knowledge cutoff).
- **Adaptation:** AI must evolve with changing environments (e.g., fraud detection in finance).

Example:

- Self-driving cars improve by continuously learning from new road scenarios.

5. DATA GOVERNANCE IS AI GOVERNANCE

Strong **data** **governance** ensures:

✓ **High-quality training data** → Accurate AI

✓ **Bias detection & mitigation** → Fair AI

✓ **Regulatory compliance** → Trustworthy AI

✓ **Traceability & auditability** → Explainable AI

Without proper data governance, AI governance fails.

Conclusion: Data is the Make-or-Break Factor for AI Success

- **Good Data → Smart, Fair, Reliable AI**
- **Bad Data → Flawed, Biased, Dangerous AI**

DATA GOVERNANCE AS THE FOUNDATION FOR EFFECTIVE AI GOVERNANCE

---

1. THE CRITICAL LINK BETWEEN DATA AND AI GOVERNANCE

1.1 Why Data Governance Precedes AI Governance

- **Input-Output Principle:** "Garbage in, Garbage out" - AI models amplify data quality issues exponentially

- **Regulatory Dependency:** 78% of AI compliance requirements trace back to underlying data practices

- **Model Performance Reality:** Data quality accounts for 60-80% of AI model accuracy variance

1.2 The Data-AI Governance Continuum

RAW DATA → GOVERNED DATA → TRAINING SETS → AI MODELS → DECISIONS

↑ DATA GOVERNANCE ↑   ↑ AI GOVERNANCE

2 KEY DATA GOVERNANCE COMPONENTS FOR AI SYSTEMS

2.1 Foundational Elements

Data Governance Area	AI Governance Impact	Failure Consequences
Data Lineage	Model explainability requirements	Unexplainable AI decisions
Metadata Management	Feature engineering traceability	Untrackable bias sources
Quality Standards	Model performance consistency	Erratic predictions
Access Controls	Model security protections	Adversarial attacks

2.2 Specialized AI Data Requirements

a) Training Data Governance:

- **Bias Mitigation:** Must document demographic distributions in training sets
- **Version Control:** Require immutable dataset snapshots tied to model versions
- **Provenance Tracking:** Need complete chain of custody from source to model

b) Production Data Governance:

- **Drift Monitoring:** Implement statistical process control for input data
- **Feedback Loops:** Structured mechanisms for label corrections
- **Anomaly Detection:** Real-time data quality gates before inference

3. OPERATIONAL FRAMEWORK FOR AI-READY DATA GOVERNANCE

3.1 Critical Control Points

1. **Ingestion Layer:**
   - Data contracts for all sources
   - Automated quality scoring ($\geq$90% threshold)
2. **Transformation Layer:**
   - Feature store governance
   - Dimensionality reduction audits
3. **Serving Layer:**

- o   Inference data validation
- o   Prediction logging standards

4. REGULATORY ALIGNMENT

4.1 Global Requirements Matrix

Regulation	Data Requirement	AI Governance Implication
GDPR	Right to explanation	Document training data characteristics
EU AI Act	High-risk data standards	Implement enhanced quality controls
CCPA	Data deletion rights	Build model retraining protocols
HIPAA	De-identification	Develop specialized NLP safeguards

4.2 Compliance Architecture

AI GOVERNANCE BOARD
```
            |
+-----------+-----------+
   |                 |
```
DATA PROTECTION OFFICER   AI ETHICS COMMITTEE
```
     |               |
```
DATA QUALITY FRAMEWORK   MODEL AUDIT FRAMEWORK

5. IMPLEMENTING EFFECTIVE CONTROLS

5.1 Technical Enablers

a) Metadata Management:

- **Minimum Requirements:**
    - o 100% of training data documented
    - o ≥ 3 levels of transformation lineage
    - o Automated freshness indicators

b) Quality Monitoring:

- **Thresholds:**
    - o $\leq 2\%$ missing values for critical features
    - o $\leq 5\%$ statistical drift between versions
    - o $\geq 99\%$ schema consistency

6. MATURITY ASSESSMENT

6.1 Capability Progression

Level	Data Governance	AI Governance Readiness
1	Ad hoc	AI projects frequently fail
2	Documented	Basic model monitoring
3	Measured	Controlled AI deployment
4	Optimized	Predictive governance
5	Autonomous	Self-correcting systems

6.2 IMPLEMENTATION ROADMAP

1. **Phase 1 (0-6 months):**
    - o Inventory all AI-relevant data assets
    - o Implement basic quality controls

2. **Phase 2 (6-12 months):**

- o Build feature store with governance
- o Establish model-data lineage

3. **Phase 3 (12-18 months):**
   - o Deploy automated drift detection
   - o Integrate with AI governance tools

7. INDUSTRY-SPECIFIC CONSIDERATIONS

7.1 Financial Services

- **Focus:** Transaction data integrity
- **Special Requirement:** Time-series consistency checks
- **Tool Example:** Databricks Lakehouse for fraud detection

7.2 Healthcare

- **Focus:** PHI de-identification
- **Special Requirement:** Clinical concept mapping
- **Tool Example:** NVIDIA CLARA for medical imaging

8. EMERGING CHALLENGES

1. **Synthetic Data Governance:**
   - o Provenance tracking for generated data
   - o Quality validation approaches

2. **Edge AI Data Controls:**
   - o Distributed quality monitoring
   - o Federated learning governance

3. **Multimodal Data:**
   - o Cross-modal consistency checks
   - o Unified governance frameworks

1. **Start with Data:**
   - o 92% of AI failures originate from data issues
   - o Implement data quality SLAs before model development

2. **Build Traceability:**
   - o Require complete model-to-data lineage
   - o Use tools like MLflow + Collibra integration

3. **Measure Continuously:**
   - o Monitor both data and model metrics
   - o Establish joint data-AI governance KPIs

Governance Frameworks

1. AI FRAMEWORKS VS. AI REGULATIONS: KEY DIFFERENCES

Aspect	AI Frameworks	AI Regulations
Nature	Guidelines, best practices, or voluntary standards	Legally binding rules enforced by governments
Purpose	Help organizations	Ensure compliance

	implement AI responsibly	and mitigate societal risks
Enforcement	Voluntary adoption	Mandatory, with penalties for non-compliance
Flexibility	Adaptable to different contexts	Rigid, with defined legal requirements
Examples	NIST AI RMF, OECD AI Principles	EU AI Act, U.S. AI Executive Order

2. AI FRAMEWORKS (GUIDELINES & BEST PRACTICES)
DEFINITION:

- Structured approaches to **design, deploy, and manage AI responsibly.**
- Provide **tools, checklists, and methodologies** but are **not legally required.**

Key Characteristics:

✓ **Voluntary adoption** (companies choose to follow)

✓ **Flexible implementation** (can be tailored to industry needs)

✓ **Focus on best practices** (ethics, fairness, transparency)

Examples:

- **NIST AI Risk Management Framework (RMF)** (U.S.)
- **OECD AI Principles** (International)
- **IEEE Ethically Aligned Design** (Technical standards)
- **Corporate AI Ethics Guidelines** (e.g., Google's AI Principles)

Use Case:

A bank uses the **NIST AI RMF** to assess risks in its loan-approval AI system, even though not legally required.

3. AI REGULATIONS (LAWS & COMPLIANCE RULES)
DEFINITION:

- **Government-imposed laws** that mandate how AI must be developed and used.
- **Non-compliance results in fines, bans, or legal action.**

Key Characteristics:

✓ **Legally binding** (must be followed)

✓ **Strict requirements** (e.g., transparency, bias testing)

✓ **Enforcement mechanisms** (audits, penalties)

Examples:

- **EU AI Act** (Bans certain AI uses, requires risk assessments)
- **U.S. AI Executive Order 2023** (Safety testing for powerful AI models)
- **China's AI Regulations** (Strict rules on generative AI)
- **GDPR (for AI data privacy)** (EU)

Use Case:

A healthcare AI company **must comply** with the **EU AI Act's** high-risk AI rules or face **fines up to 7% of global revenue**.

4. How They Work Together

While **AI frameworks guide best practices, AI regulations enforce minimum standards**.

Example Workflow:

1. A company follows the **OECD AI Principles** (framework) to design a fair hiring AI.
2. The same company **must comply** with the **EU AI Act** (regulation) by conducting bias audits.

Synergy:

- **Frameworks** help companies **exceed** regulatory requirements.
- **Regulations** ensure **minimum safeguards** are met.

4. Key Takeaways

AI Frameworks	AI Regulations
Voluntary	Mandatory
Best practices	Legal requirements
Flexible	Rigid
E.g., NIST RMF, OECD	E.g., EU AI Act, U.S. Order

NIST AI Risk Management Framework (RMF) (U.S.)

Developed by: National Institute of Standards and Technology (U.S. Department of Commerce)

Release Date: January 2023

Type: Voluntary framework for managing AI risks

Core Structure:

- **Key Functions:**
    1. **Govern** - Establish organizational culture/policies

129

2. **Map** - Contextualize AI system risks

3. **Measure** - Assess risks quantitatively/qualitatively

4. **Manage** - Implement risk mitigation strategies

Characteristics of Trustworthy AI:

• Valid and reliable • Safe • Secure • Accountable • Explainable • Fair (with harmful bias managed)

Implementation Tools:

- **Playbook** with 700+ actionable recommendations

- **Sector-specific profiles** (healthcare, finance, etc.)

- **AI Risk Scoring methodology**

Best For: Organizations needing a technical, measurable approach to AI risk

---

2. OECD AI Principles (International)

Adopted by: 38 OECD countries + non-member signatories

First Published: 2019

Type: High-level policy framework

5 Core Principles:

1. **Inclusive growth** - AI should benefit people/planet

2. **Human-centered values** - Respect human rights/democracy

3. **Transparency** - Disclose when AI is being used

4. **Robustness/Safety** - Function reliably without harm

5. **Accountability** - Clear responsibility for AI outcomes

Implementation Guidance:

- **OECD AI Policy Observatory** tracks national implementations
- **Country-specific adoption:**
  - ○ Japan: Incorporated into Social Principles of Human-Centric AI
  - ○ EU: Influenced the AI Act's risk-based approach

Best For: Policymakers and multinational corporations

---

3. IEEE Ethically Aligned Design (Technical Standards)

Developed by: IEEE Standards Association

Latest Version: EADv2 (2023)

Type: Technical implementation standards

Key Components:

- **73 Standards Projects** including:
  - • P7001 - Transparency of autonomous systems
  - • P7002 - Data privacy process standards
  - • P7009 - Anti-bias standards for AI systems
- **Certification Programs:**
  - • Algorithmic bias assessment
  - • AI system safety marking

Technical Requirements Examples:

- **P7001 Transparency:** Must document:
  - System capabilities/limitations
  - Accuracy rates per demographic group
  - Training data sources

Best For: Engineers needing technical specs for ethical AI development

---

4. Corporate AI Ethics Guidelines (Google's Principles Example)

First Published: 2018 (Updated 2023)

Type: Voluntary corporate policy

Google's 7 AI Principles:

1. **Be socially beneficial**
2. **Avoid creating/reinforcing bias**
3. **Be built/tested for safety**
4. **Be accountable to people**
5. **Incorporate privacy design**
6. **Uphold scientific excellence**
7. **Be made available for uses that accord with these principles**

Implementation Mechanisms:

- **Advanced Technology Review Council** (ATRC):
  - Reviews sensitive AI projects
  - Has blocked AI applications violating principles
- **Responsible AI Practices:**
  - Model Cards for transparency
  - What-If Tool for bias testing

Best For: Tech companies building consumer-facing AI products

Comparative Analysis Table

Framewo rk	Scope	Binding?	Key Strength	Implementat ion Level
NIST RMF	Risk managem ent	No	Detailed risk scoring	Operational
OECD	Policy principles	No (but adopted by government s)	Global alignment	Strategic

| IEEE | Technical standards | Voluntary certification | Engineering specs | Technical |
| Google | Corporate ethics | Internal enforcement | Product-level guardrails | Organizational |

IMPLEMENTATION ROADMAP FOR ORGANIZATIONS

1. **Start with OECD Principles** for strategic alignment
2. **Adopt NIST RMF** for risk management processes
3. **Apply IEEE Standards** for technical development
4. **Develop internal guidelines** (like Google's) for culture

   Tools to Operationalize:

- NIST's **AI RMF Playbook**
- IEEE's **Certification Programs**
- Google's **Responsible AI Toolkit**

Regulatory landscapes

INTRODUCTION TO AI REGULATORY LANDSCAPES: A GLOBAL OVERVIEW

The rapid advancement of artificial intelligence (AI) has prompted governments worldwide to develop **regulatory frameworks** to ensure **ethical, safe, and accountable** AI deployment. Unlike voluntary guidelines, these regulations carry **legal consequences** for non-compliance, shaping how organizations design, deploy, and monitor AI systems.

KEY DRIVERS OF AI REGULATION

1. **Risk Mitigation** – Preventing harm from biased, unsafe, or manipulative AI.

2. **Human Rights Protection** – Ensuring AI respects privacy, fairness, and autonomy.

3. **Economic & National Security** – Maintaining competitiveness while preventing misuse.

4. **Public Trust** – Building confidence in AI through transparency and accountability.

Global Regulatory Approaches

Region	Key Regulation	Focus	Enforcement
European Union	EU AI Act (2024)	Risk-based tiers	Fines up to **7% of global revenue**
United States	AI Executive Order (2023)	Safety testing, transparency	Sectoral enforcement

			(FTC, FDA)
China	AI Regulations (2023)	Content control, security	Strict licensing & audits
Canada	AIDA (2023)	High-impact AI systems	Fines up to **5% of revenue**
Brazil	AI Bill (2024)	Human rights, risk-based	Proposed oversight body

The EU AI Act: A Comprehensive Guide to the World's First AI Law

1. OVERVIEW & SIGNIFICANCE

The **EU AI Act** (formally adopted May 2024) is the **world's first comprehensive AI regulation**, establishing a legal framework for AI systems across the European Union. This landmark legislation:

- Takes a **risk-based approach**, classifying AI systems by potential harm

- Applies to **all organizations** (EU-based or foreign) offering AI in the EU market
- Introduces **stiff penalties** (up to €35M or 7% global revenue)
- Serves as a **global benchmark**, similar to GDPR's impact on data privacy

2. RISK-BASED CLASSIFICATION SYSTEM

Risk Tier	Examples	Requirements	Timeline
Unacceptable Risk (Banned)	Social scoring, emotion recognition in workplaces, predictive policing	**Total prohibition**	Immediate ban (2024)
High-Risk	Medical devices, critical infrastructure, education, law enforcement	Conformity assessments, human oversight, logging	2025-2026
Limited Risk	Chatbots, deepfakes	Transparency disclosures (e.g., "This is AI-generated")	2025

Minimal Risk	Spam filters, video games	No restrictions	N/A

3. KEY REQUIREMENTS FOR HIGH-RISK AI

3.1 Governance & Documentation

- **Fundamental Rights Impact Assessment** (FRIA)
- **Technical Documentation** (training data, algorithms)
- **Quality Management System** (ISO 13485-like for AI)
- **Human Oversight** (must be able to override decisions)

3.2 Technical Compliance

- **Risk Management System** (continuous monitoring)
- **Data Governance** (representative training datasets)
- **Accuracy/ Robustness Standards** (performance metrics)
- **Cybersecurity Protections** (penetration testing)

3.3 Transparency Obligations

- **User Notifications** (when interacting with AI)
- **Authorized Representative** (for non-EU providers)
- **Public Register** of high-risk AI systems

4. SPECIAL RULES FOR FOUNDATION MODELS

Additional requirements for **general-purpose AI (GPAI)** models like GPT:

- **Model Evaluations** (pre-market & post-market)
- **Systemic Risk Monitoring** (for "very capable" models)
- **Disclosure of Training Data** (copyright compliance)
- **Energy Efficiency Reporting**

5. ENFORCEMENT & PENALTIES

Violation Type	Fine (Higher of)	Examples
Banned AI Use	€35M or 7% revenue	Social scoring systems
High-Risk Non-Compliance	€15M or 3% revenue	Missing conformity assessment
Documentation Failures	€7.5M or 1.5% revenue	Incomplete technical docs
Misinformation	€7.5M or 1.5% revenue	Undisclosed deepfakes

Enforcement Bodies:

- National market surveillance authorities
- New **European AI Office** for GPAI oversight
- **Notified Bodies** for conformity assessments

6. IMPLEMENTATION TIMELINE

Date	Milestone
May 2024	Final adoption
Q3 2024	First bans apply
2025	High-risk rules phase in
2026	Full enforcement
2027	Review clause activation

7. BUSINESS IMPLICATIONS

For AI Providers:

- **Compliance Costs:** Estimated €50K-500K per high-risk system
- **Market Access:** CE marking required for high-risk AI
- **Liability:** New EU product liability rules apply

For Users:

- Right to explanation for AI decisions
- Bans on certain employee monitoring AI
- Mandatory AI impact assessments in public sector

8. Global Impact

- **Brussels Effect:** Likely to set global standards (like GDPR)
- **US Companies:** Must comply for EU market access
- **Third Countries:** Japan, Canada aligning laws

9. Compliance Checklist

1. Classify your AI system's risk level
2. Conduct gap analysis against requirements
3. Develop technical documentation
4. Implement risk management system
5. Appoint EU representative (if non-EU based)
6. Register high-risk systems in EU database

Next Steps for Organizations:

- Map existing AI systems to risk categories
- Begin FRIA for high-risk applications
- Monitor delegated acts for sector-specific rules

U.S. AI Regulations: A Comprehensive Guide

1. OVERVIEW OF THE U.S. REGULATORY LANDSCAPE

Unlike the EU's unified AI Act, the U.S. takes a **sectoral approach** to AI regulation, combining:

- **Federal agency actions** (FTC, FDA, etc.)
- **State laws** (California, Colorado, etc.)
- **White House executive orders**
- **Voluntary frameworks** (NIST AI RMF)

2. Key Federal Regulations & Policies

2.1 Biden's AI Executive Order (Oct 2023)

Scope: Applies to federal agencies and companies working with them

Key Requirements:

- **Safety Testing:** Developers of powerful AI systems must share results with government
- **Privacy Protections:** Strengthened guidance for AI using personal data
- **Civil Rights:** Address algorithmic discrimination in housing, employment, etc.
- **Workforce Impact:** Labor standards for AI-augmented jobs
- **National Security:** Cloud provider reporting of foreign

AI training

Enforcement: Through federal procurement rules and agency powers

2.2 Sector-Specific Regulations

Sector	Agency	Key Rules
Healthcare	FDA	AI/ML-based SaMD Pre-Cert Program (2023)
Finance	SEC, CFPB	Algorithmic trading disclosures (2024)
Employment	EEOC	Guidance on AI in hiring (May 2023)
Consumer	FTC	Warning about deceptive AI practices

2.3 Proposed Federal Legislation

- **AI Foundation Model Transparency Act** (required disclosures)
- **Algorithmic Accountability Act** (impact assessments)
- **NO FAKES Act** (AI voice/image protections)

3. STATE-LEVEL AI LAWS

3.1 California

- **Delete Act** (2023): Allows deletion of personal data used in AI
- **Draft AI Regulations:** Risk assessments for "consequential" AI

3.2 Colorado

- **AI Insurance Law** (2024): Bans discriminatory

algorithms

3.3 Illinois

- **AI Video Interview Act** (2020): Consent requirements

4. ENFORCEMENT MECHANISMS

- **FTC Act Section 5:** Unfair/deceptive practices ($50K/violation)
- **Civil Rights Laws:** DOJ actions for discriminatory AI
- **Sectoral Regulators:** FDA recalls for unsafe medical AI

5. COMPLIANCE FRAMEWORK

5.1 Mandatory Requirements

- **Safety Testing** for powerful models
- **Bias Audits** in regulated sectors
- **Transparency Disclosures** in some states

5.2 Recommended Practices

1. Implement **NIST AI RMF**
2. Conduct **algorithmic impact assessments**
3. Maintain **model documentation**
4. Establish **AI governance committees**

6. COMPARISON WITH EU AI ACT

Aspect	U.S. Approach	EU AI Act
Structure	Sectoral agencies	Unified law
Risk Basis	Case-by-case	Tiered system
Penalties	Vary by agency	Up to 7% revenue
Focus	Innovation + safety	Precautionary

7. Business Implications

- **Federal Contractors:** Strictest compliance burdens

- **Healthcare/Finance:** Most regulated sectors

- **Generative AI:** Emerging disclosure rules

- **All Companies:** Rising litigation risks

China: Strict AI Governance with Tiered Oversight

Key Regulations:

- **Interim Measures for Generative AI (2023) –** Focuses on deepfakes and synthetic content.

- **Algorithmic Recommendations Regulation (2022) –** Requires transparency and user opt-outs.

- **New AI Law (Draft, 2024) –** Expands to general-purpose AI (e.g., foundation models).

Requirements:

- **Security Assessments:** Mandatory government reviews for public-facing AI.

- **Data Localization:** AI training data must be stored in China.
- **Content Controls:** AI must align with "socialist core values."

Enforcement:

- Fines up to **¥100M (~$14M)** for violations.
- **Cyberspace Administration of China (CAC)** conducts audits.

Example: *Baidu's Ernie Bot* underwent security reviews before public release.

---

2. Canada: Proactive Risk-Based Framework

Key Regulation:

- **Artificial Intelligence and Data Act (AIDA, 2023)** – Part of Bill C-27.

Risk Tiers:

- **High-Impact AI:** Requires assessments, transparency, and mitigation plans.
- **General AI:** Voluntary compliance with guidelines.

Requirements:

- **Impact Assessments:** For AI used in hiring, healthcare, etc.
- **Human Oversight:** Critical decisions must have human

review.

- **Public Disclosure:** Deployers must notify users when AI is used.

Enforcement:

- Fines up to **5%** of **global revenue** or **CAD $25M** (whichever is higher).

- **Office of the AI and Data Commissioner** oversees compliance.

Example: *Shopify* must comply with AIDA for its AI-powered recommendation tools.

---

3. Brazil: Human-Centric AI Rules

Key Regulation:

- **AI Bill (PL 21/2020, expected 2024)** – Inspired by EU AI Act but adapted to local needs.

Key Rules:

- **Risk-Based Categories:** Similar to EU (unacceptable/high/limited/minimal risk).

- **Bias Mitigation:** Requires testing for racial/gender bias (critical for public services).

- **Right to Explanation:** Users can request AI decision rationale.

Enforcement:

- **National AI Authority** will oversee compliance.
- Fines up to **2% of Brazilian revenue**.

Example: *Nubank* must audit its credit-scoring AI for bias under the new law.

---

4. Japan: Flexible Guidelines with Incentives

Key Regulation:

- **Social Principles of Human-Centric AI (2022)** – Non-binding but influential.
- **AI Business Guidelines (2023)** – Sector-specific recommendations.

Focus Areas:

- **Transparency:** Disclose AI limitations (e.g., SoftBank's customer service bots).
- **Innovation Support:** Tax incentives for ethical AI R&D.

Enforcement:

- No fines, but **market pressure** drives compliance (e.g., lost contracts).

- **Ministry of Economy, Trade and Industry (METI)** provides certifications.

Example: *Toyota* follows METI's guidelines for autonomous vehicle AI.

---

5. Singapore: Pro-Business with Strong Governance

Key Regulation:

- **AI Verify (2022)** – Government-backed toolkit for responsible AI.

- **Model AI Governance Framework (2020)** – Voluntary but widely adopted.

Requirements:

- **Explainability:** Document decision-making processes.

- **Fairness Testing:** For financial/HR AI systems.

- **Data Accountability:** Maintain audit trails.

Enforcement:

- **Monetary Authority of Singapore (MAS)** mandates AI governance in finance.

148

- No fines, but non-compliance risks **loss of government contracts**.

Example: *DBS Bank* uses AI Verify for its loan approval systems.

---

6. UAE & Saudi Arabia: Gulf-Specific AI Laws

Key Regulations:

- **UAE National AI Strategy 2031** – Focuses on economic growth.
- **Saudi Data & AI Authority (SDAIA) Regulations** – Requires government approval for high-risk AI.

Requirements:

- **Local Data Storage:** Training data must reside in-country.
- **Cultural Alignment:** AI must respect Islamic values.
- **Pilot Testing:** Mandatory for public-sector AI.

Enforcement:

- **SDAIA** (Saudi) and **Dubai AI Ethics Advisory Board** (UAE) monitor compliance.

149

- Violators face **suspension of AI services**.

Example: *G42 Healthcare* (UAE) complies with local data rules for diagnostic AI.

---

7. India: Emerging Regulatory Framework

Key Regulation:

- **Digital India Act (2024, draft)** – Includes AI governance provisions.

Proposed Rules:

- **Mandatory Labeling:** For deepfakes and synthetic media.

- **Sectoral Oversight:** Healthcare, finance, and education AI will face stricter rules.

Enforcement (Expected):

- **Ministry of Electronics and IT (MeitY)** will oversee compliance.

- Fines up to ☐**50M (~$600K)** for violations.

Example: *Zomato's* food recommendation AI may need bias audits under new rules.

Comparative Summary: Global AI Regulations

Country	Key Law	Risk Approach	Max Fine	Enforcement Body
China	Generative AI Rules	Content-focused	$14M	CAC
Canada	AIDA	High-impact focus	5% revenue	AI Commissioner
Brazil	AI Bill (2024)	EU-style tiers	2% revenue	National AI Authority
Japan	METI Guideline	Voluntary	None	METI

	s			
Singapore	AI Verify	Toolkit-based	Contract loss	IMDA
UAE/Saudi	SDAIA Rules	Cultural alignment	Service ban	SDAIA
India	Digital India Act	Sectoral	$600	MeitY

KEY TAKEAWAYS FOR BUSINESSES

1. **China & Brazil** mirror the EU's strictness, while **Japan & Singapore** prefer guidelines.
2. **Canada's AIDA** is the closest to the EU AI Act in structure.
3. **Gulf countries** emphasize data localization and cultural compliance.
4. **India's** rules are still evolving but will likely target deepfakes first.

Next Steps for Compliance:

- Map AI use cases to local risk categories.
- Conduct bias/impact assessments where required.
- Monitor for new laws (especially in India and Brazil).

Public-Private Partnerships

1. Definition & Importance of AI PPPs

What Are AI PPPs?
Collaborations between governments, private companies, and academia to accelerate **responsible AI development and deployment** while addressing societal challenges.

Why They Matter:

- Bridge gaps in funding, data access, and expertise
- Align AI innovation with public interest (e.g., healthcare, climate)
- Mitigate risks through shared governance frameworks

2. TYPES OF AI PPPS

Type	Objective	Examples
Research & Development	Joint AI innovation	*EU's CLAIRE (Confederation of Labs*

		for AI Research in Europe)
Data Sharing	Secure access to public/private datasets	*UK's NHS-DeepMind Health partnership*
Policy Sandboxes	Test AI regulations in controlled environments	*Singapore's AI Verify Foundation*
Talent Development	Upskill workforce for AI jobs	*U.S. National AI Research Resource (NAIRR)*
Crisis Response	Deploy AI for emergencies	*WHO's AI-powered pandemic forecasting with Google*

3. KEY GLOBAL AI PPP INITIATIVES

3.1 United States

- **National AI Research Resource (NAIRR)**
    - o **Partners:** NSF, NVIDIA, OpenAI, Anthropic
    - o **Goal:** Provide researchers with compute power and public datasets
    - o **Funding:** $2.6B over 5 years (CHIPS Act)
- **AI Safety Institute Consortium (AISIC)**
    - o **Partners:** NIST, Microsoft, Google, Apple

- o **Goal:** Develop AI safety standards (aligned with Biden's EO)

3.2 EUROPEAN UNION

- **European AI Alliance**
  - o **Partners:** EU Commission, SAP, Bosch
  - o **Goal:** Implement ethical guidelines from the EU AI Act
- **GAIA-X** (European Cloud/AI Infrastructure)
  - o **Partners:** Deutsche Telekom, Siemens, AWS
  - o **Goal:** Reduce dependency on U.S./Chinese cloud providers

3.3 Asia

- **Japan's Moonshot R&D Program**
  - o **Partners:** Toyota, Fujitsu, Tokyo University
  - o **Goal:** Develop "symbiotic" AI for aging society support
- **India's AI Mission (□10,300Cr Fund)**
  - o **Partners:** Infosys, NASSCOM, IITs
  - o **Goal:** Build sovereign AI for healthcare and agriculture

4. BENEFITS OF AI PPPs

✅ **For Governments:**

- Access to cutting-edge tech without full R&D costs
- Faster policy implementation (e.g., smart cities)

✅ **For Companies:**

- Shared risk in high-stakes AI projects
- Priority access to public datasets (e.g., traffic, health records)

☑ **For Society:**

- AI solutions for public goods (e.g., disaster prediction)
- Job creation through reskilling programs

5. CHALLENGES & RISKS

Data Privacy: Balancing open innovation with GDPR-style protections

IP Ownership: Disputes over who controls jointly developed AI

Vendor Lock-in: Over-reliance on big tech (e.g., AWS in government clouds)

Equity Gaps: SMEs often excluded from high-value partnerships

Case Study:

- **IBM-Watson & MD Anderson Cancer Center**
  - **Goal:** AI for oncology treatment recommendations
  - **Failure Reason:** Poor data integration and unclear ROI led to $62M loss

6. BEST PRACTICES FOR SUCCESSFUL AI PPPS

1. **Define Clear KPIs Early** (e.g., accuracy benchmarks, public impact metrics)
2. **Use Neutral Data Trusts** to enable secure sharing (e.g., UK's ODI models)
3. **Adopt Modular Contracts** to adjust scope as tech evolves
4. **Include Civil Society** (e.g., AI Now Institute in NYC's algorithmic audits)

AI GOVERNANCE IN PRACTICE

Navigating the Age of AI

NAVIGATING THE AGE OF AI: A STEP-BY-STEP GUIDE TO AI GOVERNANCE IMPLEMENTATION

1. UNDERSTANDING AI GOVERNANCE

AI Governance refers to the frameworks, policies, and practices that ensure AI systems are developed and deployed **responsibly, ethically, and legally**. It addresses:

Risk Management (bias, security, misuse)

Regulatory Compliance (GDPR, EU AI Act, U.S. Executive Orders)

Ethical Alignment (fairness, transparency, accountability)

2. KEY PILLARS OF AI GOVERNANCE IMPLEMENTATION

2.1 Strategic Alignment

- **Define AI Principles** (e.g., Google's AI Ethics, Microsoft's Responsible AI)

- **Establish Governance Structure**:
  - **AI Ethics Board** (cross-functional: legal, tech, business)
  - **Chief AI Officer** (oversees compliance)
- **Map AI Use Cases to Risk Levels** (e.g., EU AI Act's *prohibited/high/limited risk* tiers)

2.2 Policy & Process Development

- **AI Policy Framework**
  - Data governance (quality, privacy, bias mitigation)
  - Model lifecycle management (development → deployment → monitoring)
- **Risk Assessment Protocols**
  - **Bias Audits** (e.g., IBM's *AI Fairness 360*)
  - **Security Testing** (adversarial attacks, data leaks)

2.3 Technical Implementation

- **Tools for Compliance:**

Requirement	Tool Examples
Explainability	SHAP, LIME, InterpretML
Bias Detection	Fairlearn, Aequitas
Model Monitoring	Evidently AI, Fiddler AI
Data Governance	Collibra, Alation

- **Documentation Standards:**

160

- Model Cards (Google's format)
- Data Sheets (provenance, demographics)

2.4 Compliance & Monitoring

- **Regulatory Mapping**
  - **EU AI Act**: Conformity assessments for high-risk AI
  - **U.S. NIST RMF**: Voluntary but critical for federal contracts
  - **China's AI Laws**: Data localization + content controls

- **Continuous Monitoring**
  - **Drift Detection** (statistical shifts in data/model performance)
  - **Incident Response Plan** (e.g., AI bias complaints)

3. STEP-BY-STEP IMPLEMENTATION ROADMAP

Phase 1: Assess (Weeks 1-4)

- **Audit existing AI systems** for risks (bias, security, compliance gaps)
- **Benchmark against regulations** (e.g., EU AI Act's prohibited practices)

Phase 2: Design (Weeks 5-8)

- **Draft AI governance policies** (ethics, data, model management)
- **Assign roles** (AI Ethics Board, Data Stewards)

Phase 3: Implement (Weeks 9-16)

- **Deploy technical tools** (bias detection, model monitoring)
- **Train teams** on responsible AI practices

Phase 4: Monitor (Ongoing)

- **Automated alerts** for model drift/bias
- **Quarterly compliance reviews**

4. INDUSTRY-SPECIFIC CONSIDERATIONS

Sector	Key Governance Focus	Regulatory Priority
Healthcare	Patient safety, HIPAA compliance	FDA's AI/ML-Based SaMD Framework
Finance	Anti-bias (loan approvals), AML checks	SEC Algorithmic Trading Rules
Retail	Consumer privacy, dynamic pricing ethics	California Delete Act (2023)
Defense	Autonomous weapons bans, explainability	NATO AI Principles

5. OVERCOMING COMMON CHALLENGES

- **Challenge 1: Siloed Data**

  Solution: Implement a **data trust** for secure cross-team access.

- **Challenge 2: Bias in Models**

  Solution: Pre-process training data

with **reweighting/resampling**.

- **Challenge 3: Regulatory Fragmentation**

  Solution: Adopt **NIST AI RMF** as a baseline, then layer local laws.

6. FUTURE-PROOFING AI GOVERNANCE

- **AI Governance Automation** (e.g., AI monitoring AI)
- **Global Standardization** (ISO 42001 certification)
- **Quantum AI Governance** (preparing for post-quantum cryptography risks)

Key Takeaways

1. Start with a **risk assessment** of AI systems.
2. Combine **policy + tools** (e.g., bias audits + Fairlearn).
3. Monitor continuously—**AI governance is not one-time**.

CUSTOMIZED AI GOVERNANCE ROADMAPS FOR HEALTHCARE, BANKING & SUPPLY CHAIN

---

1. HEALTHCARE AI GOVERNANCE ROADMAP

(Focus: Patient Safety, HIPAA/GDPR Compliance, Clinical Validation)

Phase 1: Assess (Month 1-2)

- **Risk Audit**

- Classify AI uses per **EU AI Act** (e.g., diagnostic tools = *high-risk*)
- Map to **FDA's SaMD Framework** (Pre-Cert Program)

- **Data Review**
  - Ensure PHI (Protected Health Information) meets **HIPAA de-identification standards**
  - Check dataset diversity (e.g., age, gender, ethnicity for bias)

Phase 2: Design (Month 3-4)

- **Policies**
  - **Ethics Board** with clinicians, data scientists, and patient advocates
  - **Model Documentation:** FDA-style "Predetermined Change Control Plans"

- **Tools**
  - **Bias Mitigation:** IBM Watson's **Fairness 360** for diagnostic AI
  - **Explainability:** LIME/SHAP for treatment recommendation models

Phase 3: Implement (Month 5-6)

- **Pilot Testing**
  - Validate AI in controlled environments (e.g., Mayo Clinic's **AI validation labs**)
  - Use **synthetic data** for initial training (e.g., NVIDIA Clara)

- **Compliance**
  - ○ Submit **FDA 510(k)** for AI-based medical devices
  - ○ Implement **ISO 13485** (QMS for medical AI)

Phase 4: Monitor (Ongoing)

- **Real-World Performance**
  - ○ Track **false positives/negatives** in cancer detection AI
  - ○ Monitor **model drift** using Evidently AI
- **Audits**
  - ○ Annual **HIPAA security reviews**
  - ○ **Third-party bias audits** (e.g., Johns Hopkins partnership)

2. BANKING AI GOVERNANCE ROADMAP

(Focus: Anti-Bias, AML Compliance, Explainable Credit Decisions)

Phase 1: Assess (Month 1-2)

- **Regulatory Mapping**
  - ○ Align with **EU AI Act** (credit scoring = *high-risk*)
  - ○ Comply with **CFPB's Algorithmic Accountability Act** (U.S.)
- **Bias Detection**
  - ○ Test loan-approval AI for **disparate impact** (e.g., 80% rule analysis)

Phase 2: Design (Month 3-4)

- Policies
  - o **Red-lining prevention**: Ban ZIP code-based risk proxies
  - o **Transparency**: Provide **"denial reason" letters** for rejected applicants
- Tools
  - o **Fraud Detection**: FICO Falcon AI with **FATF-compliant** monitoring
  - o **Explainability**: ZestFinance's **ZAML** for credit decisions

Phase 3: Implement (Month 5-6)

- **Pilot Testing**
  - o Run **shadow mode** testing (AI + human underwriters)
  - o Use **synthetic transaction data** for AML AI training
- **Compliance**
  - o **SEC filings** for AI-driven trading algorithms
  - o **SOC 2 Type II audits** for data security

Phase 4: Monitor (Ongoing)

- **Continuous Checks**
  - o **Daily PSI (Population Stability Index)** for credit models
  - o **Quarterly fair lending audits**
- **Incident Response**
  - o **72-hour breach reporting** under NYDFS Part

500

3. Supply Chain AI Governance Roadmap

(Focus: Ethical Sourcing, Predictive Accuracy, Cyber-Resilience)

Phase 1: Assess (Month 1-2)

- **Risk Audit**
  - Classify AI uses:
    - *High-risk*: Supplier labor practice monitoring
    - *Limited-risk*: Demand forecasting
  - Review **Uyghur Forced Labor Prevention Act (UFLPA)** compliance

Phase 2: Design (Month 3-4)

- **Policies**
  - **Supplier Code of Conduct**: Audit AI for modern slavery risks
  - **Explainability**: Document **reasons for supplier blacklisting**
- **Tools**
  - **Bias Mitigation**: Toolsight AI for **geopolitical risk scoring**
  - **Resilience**: IBM's **Sterling Supply Chain Suite** with cyber-AI

Phase 3: Implement (Month 5-6)

- **Pilot Testing**
  - Simulate disruptions (e.g., **AI-driven port**

congestion alerts)

- o Test **blockchain-AI** **integration** for provenance tracking

- **Compliance**
  - o **ISO 28000 certification** for security
  - o **C-TPAT (Customs-Trade Partnership) audits**

Phase 4: Monitor (Ongoing)

- **Performance Tracking**
  - o Measure **forecasting accuracy** (MAPE <10%)
  - o Monitor **supplier diversity metrics**

- **Cyber Threat Detection**
  - o **AI-powered anomaly detection** (e.g., Darktrace)

KEY TOOLS COMPARISON

Sector	Bias Mitigation	Explainability	Compliance
Healthcare	IBM Fairness 360	LIME/SHAP	FDA 510(k)
Banking	ZestFinance ZAML	FICO Explainable AI	CFPB Audits
Supply Chain	Toolsight AI	IBM Sterling	ISO 28000

Tools for Responsible AI

ULTIMATE RESPONSIBLE AI TOOLS TOOLKIT

1. BIAS DETECTION & FAIRNESS TOOLS

2.

Tool	Type	Key Features	Best For	License
AI Fairness 360 (IBM)	Open-source Python	70+ fairness metrics, bias mitigation algorithms	Financial services, hiring	Apache 2.0
Fairlearn (Microsoft)	Open-source Python	Disparate impact analysis, visualization dashboards	Healthcare, public sector	MIT
Aequitas (UChicago)	Open-source	Bias audits for binary/multi-class	Criminal justice,	BSD

	Python	models	educatio n	
What-If Tool (Google)	GUI + Python	Interactive fairness testing for TensorFlow/PyT orch	Product teams	Apache 2.0
Biaslyze	Commerc ial SaaS	Auto-detects gender/racial bias in NLP models	HR tech, marketin g	Subscripti on

2. EXPLAINABILITY & INTERPRETABILITY

SHAP (SHapley Additive exPlanations) | Python library | Model-agnostic feature importance | Any black-box model | MIT |

LIME (Local Interpretable Model-agnostic Explanations) | Python library | Explains individual predictions | Medical diagnosis, fraud detection | BSD |

InterpretML (Microsoft) | Python library | Glass-box models + explainability dashboards | Regulatory compliance | MIT |

Alibi (Seldon) | Open-source Python | Counterfactual explanations, anchor rules | Financial approvals | Apache 2.0 |

DALEX | R/Python | Model-agnostic visual explanations | Academic research | GPL-3 |

3. MODEL MONITORING & DRIFT DETECTION

| **Evidently AI** | Open-source Python | Data drift, model

performance decay | Production AI systems | Apache 2.0 |

| **Fiddler AI** | Commercial SaaS | End-to-end model monitoring + NLP bias detection | Enterprise deployments | Subscription |

| **Aporia** | Commercial SaaS | Real-time drift alerts for tabular/NLP models | Fintech, e-commerce | Subscription |

| **Arthur AI** | Commercial SaaS | Bias + drift monitoring with human feedback loops | Government, healthcare | Subscription |

| **WhyLabs** | Freemium SaaS | Automated data quality monitoring | Startups, cloud-native | Freemium |

4. PRIVACY & SECURITY

| **TensorFlow Privacy** | Open-source Python | Differential privacy for ML training | Healthcare, public data | Apache 2.0 |

| **PySyft** (OpenMined) | Open-source Python | Federated learning + secure multi-party computation | Banking, defense | Apache 2.0 |

| **IBM Homomorphic Encryption Toolkit** | Library | Encrypted data computation | Sensitive government data | Commercial |

| **Presidio** (Microsoft) | Open-source Python | PII anonymization for text/NLP | Customer service chatbots | MIT |

| **Great Expectations** | Open-source Python | Data validation framework | Pre-training data checks | Apache 2.0 |

5. GOVERNANCE & DOCUMENTATION

Model Cards (Google)	Template	Standardized model documentation	Regulatory compliance	CC-BY 4.0
AI FactSheets (IBM)	Framework	End-to-end AI system disclosures	EU AI Act compliance	Commercial
Collibra	Commercial SaaS	Data lineage + metadata management	Enterprise governance	Subscription
Alation	Commercial SaaS	AI catalog with compliance tracking	Financial services	Subscription
Credo AI	Commercial SaaS	Policy engine for AI governance	Highly regulated industries	Subscription

6. SYNTHETIC DATA GENERATION

Synthea	Open-source Java	Synthetic patient health records	Medical AI training	Apache 2.0
Gretel.ai	Commercial SaaS	Privacy-preserving synthetic data	Customer analytics	Subscription
Mostly AI	Commercial SaaS	Tabular synthetic data generator	Banking, insurance	Subscription
NVIDIA Omniverse Replicator	SDK	Synthetic computer vision data	Autonomous vehicles	Freemium

7. COMPLIANCE & REGULATORY

| **NIST AI RMF Playbook** | Framework | Risk management guidelines | U.S. government contractors | Public Domain |
| **IBM Watson OpenScale** | Commercial SaaS | Compliance monitoring for EU AI Act | High-risk AI systems | Subscription |
| **Fairly AI** | Commercial SaaS | Automated regulatory

172

documentation | Startups scaling globally | Subscription |

| **Holistic AI** | Commercial SaaS | GDPR/HIPAA compliance audits | Healthcare, fintech | Subscription |

8. OPEN-SOURCE TOOLKITS

| **Responsible AI Toolkit** (Microsoft) | Collection | Fairness, interpretability, error analysis | End-to-end pipelines | MIT |

| **Lucent** (Google) | Open-source Python | Visualizing neural network decisions | Computer vision | Apache 2.0 |

| **DVC** (Iterative) | Open-source Python | Version control for data/models | Reproducible ML | Apache 2.0 |

| **MLflow** | Open-source Python | Model lifecycle management | Experiment tracking | Apache 2.0 |

Implementation Guide

---

1. **Start with Bias Testing** → Use **AI Fairness 360** or **Fairlearn**

2. **Add Explainability** → Deploy **SHAP/LIME** for regulators

3. **Monitor Production** → Set up **Evidently AI** or **Fiddler**

4. **Document** → Create **Model Cards** + **FactSheets**

5. **Ensure Compliance** → Run **NIST AI RMF** assessments

Case Studies of Effective Governance

Challenge: Responsible Deployment of AI-Powered Loan Approval System

A global bank with operations in 30+ countries needs to:

- Automate loan decisions while preventing bias
- Comply with EU AI Act (high-risk), U.S. ECOA, and other regulations
- Maintain customer trust through transparency

6-STEP AI GOVERNANCE IMPLEMENTATION

175

1. ESTABLISH GOVERNANCE STRUCTURE

Example Implementation:

- Formed **AI Ethics Board** with:
    - Chief Risk Officer (Chair)
    - Head of Data Science
    - Chief Compliance Officer
    - External ethicist (Harvard Law Professor)
    - Consumer advocacy representative

Output:

AI Governance Charter defining:

- Risk thresholds (e.g., max 5% approval rate variance across demographics)
- Escalation paths for ethical concerns

2. RISK ASSESSMENT & CLASSIFICATION

Applied Framework:

EU AI Act's high-risk classification + NIST AI RMF

Process:

1. Mapped loan approval AI to requirements:
    - ✅ High-risk (credit scoring affects livelihoods)
    - ✅ Requires conformity assessment
2. Conducted bias audit:
    - Found 8% lower approval rates for immigrant applicants

Tool: IBM AI Fairness 360 (disparate impact ratio = 0.76 → requires mitigation)

3. TECHNICAL SAFEGUARDS IMPLEMENTATION

Solutions Deployed:

Risk	Mitigation	Tool
Bias	Added alternative data (utility payments) + reweighting	Aequitas
Opacity	SHAP explanations for all denials	InterpretML
Drift	Monthly PSI monitoring	Fiddler AI
Security	Homomorphic encryption for sensitive data	Microsoft SEAL

Model Card Excerpt:

Training Data: 2M applications (2018-2023)

Demographics: 52% male, 48% female; 12% immigrants

Accuracy: 88% (vs. 82% human baseline)

Known Limitations: Lower confidence for gig economy workers

4. COMPLIANCE INTEGRATION

Regulatory Alignment:

- **EU AI Act:** Full technical documentation submitted
- **U.S. ECOA:** Monthly fair lending reports to CFPB
- **GDPR:** Right to explanation workflow implemented

Process   Change:

Loan officers now:

1. Review all AI denials
2. Can override with justification (logged in system)
3. Provide applicants with:
   - Reason for denial (SHAP output)

o   Appeal process

5. MONITORING & CONTINUOUS IMPROVEMENT

Dashboard Metrics:

- Daily: Approval rates by demographic
- Weekly: PSI scores for input data
- Monthly: False positive/negative analysis

Incident Example:

- March 2024: Detected 2% drift in self-employed applicant approvals
- Action: Retrained model + expanded training data

6. CULTURE & TRAINING

Programs Implemented:

1. **Responsible AI Certification** (80% of tech staff certified)
2. **Red Team Exercises** (quarterly bias testing)
3. **Transparency Reports** (published annually)

Results After 12 Months

Metric	Before	After
Approval bias gap	8%	2%
Processing time	5 days	2 hours
Regulatory fines	$3.2M/year	$0

Customer trust score	68/100	89/100

Key Success Factors

1. **Top-Down Commitment:** CEO tied 20% of bonuses to AI ethics KPIs
2. **Toolchain Integration:** Built governance into existing ML pipelines
3. **Regulatory Proactivity:** Engaged regulators during development

---

Case Study: Implementing AI Governance for a Hospital's Diagnostic Imaging System

---

CHALLENGE: DEPLOYING RADIOLOGY AI WHILE ENSURING PATIENT SAFETY

A 500-bed teaching hospital sought to implement an AI system for detecting lung cancer in CT scans while:

- Maintaining diagnostic accuracy ≥95% (FDA Class II device threshold)
- Preventing bias across demographic groups
- Complying with HIPAA/GDPR and EU AI Act (high-risk classification)

- Preserving radiologist oversight

1. GOVERNANCE STRUCTURE ESTABLISHMENT

Implementation:

- Formed **Multidisciplinary AI Oversight Committee**:
    - Chief Medical Officer (Chair)
    - Lead Radiologist
    - Data Protection Officer
    - AI Ethics Specialist (external consultant)
    - Patient Advocate (lung cancer survivor)

Outputs:

- *AI Clinical Use Policy* mandating:
    - All AI findings require radiologist confirmation
    - Weekly quality assurance rounds
    - Immediate reporting of false negatives

2. RISK ASSESSMENT & VALIDATION

Process:

1. Classified as **high-risk** under EU AI Act/MDR and **FDA SaMD**
2. Conducted **multi-stage validation**:
    - Phase 1: 10,000 historical scans (98.2% sensitivity)
    - Phase 2: Prospective trial (96.4% real-world accuracy)
    - Phase 3: Bias testing (found 4% lower sensitivity in Black patients)

Tools Used:

- **NVIDIA Clara** for synthetic data augmentation
- **IBM Watson OpenScale** for bias detection

3. TECHNICAL SAFEGUARDS

System Architecture:

A[CT Scan] --> B[AI Analysis]

B --> C{Confidence >95%?}

C -->|Yes| D[Radiologist Review Queue]

C -->|No| E[Urgent Human Review]

D --> F[Final Diagnosis]

Key Features:

- **Explainability**: Integrated LIME visualizations showing detection regions
- **Fallback Protocol**: Auto-escalates indeterminate cases
- **Data Protection**: Federated learning across hospitals (Owkin platform)

4. COMPLIANCE INTEGRATION

Regulatory Alignment:

1. **FDA 510(k) Clearance**:
   - Submitted 287-page technical file
   - Included bias mitigation plan

2. **GDPR/HIPAA**:
   - Pseudonymization via **Microsoft Presidio**
   - Audit trails for all data accesses

Consent Workflow:

- Allow AI analysis of my scans (opt-in)

- Share anonymized data for research (opt-in)

5. MONITORING & QUALITY CONTROL

Real-Time Dashboards:

- **Clinical Operations Center** displays:
    - Daily false negative rate (<2% threshold)
    - Demographic parity metrics
    - System uptime (99.99% SLA)

Incident Response Example:

- Detected 1.8% sensitivity drop in female patients (Week 6)
- Action: Retrained with 5,000 additional female scans

6. TRAINING & CULTURE CHANGE

Programs Implemented:

1. **AI Clinician Certification:**
    - 4-hour training on:
        - Interpreting AI outputs
        - Recognizing system limitations
    - Required for all radiology staff
2. **Patient Education Portal:**
    - Videos explaining AI's role
    - Annotated sample reports

Results After 18 Months

Metric	Baseline	Post-Implementation
Cancer detection rate	91%	96%

Time to diagnosis	5.2 days	1.1 days
Racial detection gap	7%	1.5%
Radiologist workload	100%	68%
HIPAA violations	3/year	0

Key Success Factors

1. **Clinical Integration**: AI outputs embedded directly in PACS workflow

2. **Continuous Validation**: Monthly testing with new cases

3. **Transparency**: Published model card showing:
   o Training data demographics
   o Known edge cases (e.g., rare sarcoidosis presentations)

Human Factor

Incorporating the **human factor** into AI systems is essential to ensure that AI technologies are ethical, fair, and aligned with human values. The human factor involves integrating human oversight, empathy, ethics, and decision-making into AI development and deployment. Below is a detailed explanation of **how to add the human factor in AI**, including strategies, frameworks, and examples.

How to Add the Human Factor in AI

---

1. HUMAN OVERSIGHT AND CONTROL

Human oversight ensures that AI systems are used responsibly and that humans remain in control of critical decisions.

Strategies:

1. **Human-in-the-Loop (HITL):**
    - o Humans are involved in the training, validation, and decision-making processes of AI systems.
    - o Example: A human reviews and approves AI-generated medical diagnoses before they are finalized.

2. **Human-on-the-Loop (HOTL):**
    - o Humans monitor AI systems in real-time and intervene when necessary.
    - o Example: A human operator oversees an autonomous vehicle and takes control in complex situations.

3. **Human-in-Command:**
    - o Humans have ultimate authority over AI systems and can override their decisions.
    - o Example: A judge reviews AI-generated sentencing recommendations before making a final decision.

2. ETHICAL AI DESIGN

Incorporating ethics into AI design ensures that AI systems respect human values and rights.

Strategies:

1. **Ethical Guidelines:**
    - o Develop and adhere to ethical guidelines for AI development and deployment.

o Example: Google's AI Principles emphasize avoiding harm, fairness, and accountability.

2. **Bias Mitigation**:

   o Identify and mitigate biases in data and algorithms to ensure fairness.

   o Example: Using diverse datasets and conducting bias audits for AI models.

3. **Transparency and Explainability**:

   o Ensure that AI systems are transparent and their decisions are explainable.

   o Example: Providing clear explanations for AI-driven decisions in hiring.

4. **Privacy Protection**:

   o Implement robust data privacy measures to protect user information.

   o Example: Using data anonymization techniques to protect sensitive data.

3. EMPATHY AND USER-CENTRIC DESIGN

Designing AI systems with empathy ensures that they meet user needs and provide positive experiences.

Strategies:

1. **User Research**:

   o Conduct user research to understand the needs, preferences, and pain points of users.

   o Example: Conducting surveys and interviews to gather feedback on an AI-powered customer service chatbot.

2. **User-Centric Design**:

   o Design AI systems with a focus on user experience and usability.

   o Example: Creating an intuitive interface for an AI-powered healthcare app.

3. **Emotional AI**:

   o Develop AI systems that can recognize and respond to human emotions.

   o Example: An AI-powered mental health app that provides empathetic responses to users.

4. **Inclusivity**:

   o Ensure that AI systems are accessible and beneficial to all individuals, including marginalized groups.

   o Example: Developing AI-powered educational tools that are accessible to people with disabilities.

4. COLLABORATIVE AI

Collaborative AI involves humans and AI systems working together to achieve better outcomes.

Strategies:

1. **Augmented Intelligence**:

   o Use AI to augment human capabilities rather than replace them.

   o Example: AI-powered tools that assist doctors in diagnosing diseases.

2. **Human-AI Interaction**:

- o Design AI systems that facilitate seamless interaction between humans and machines.
- o Example: Voice assistants like Alexa and Google Assistant that understand and respond to natural language.

3. **Crowdsourcing**:

- o Leverage human input to improve AI systems through crowdsourcing.
- o Example: Using platforms like Amazon Mechanical Turk to label data for training AI models.

5. ETHICAL GOVERNANCE AND ACCOUNTABILITY

Establishing ethical governance frameworks ensures that AI systems are used responsibly and that accountability is maintained.

Strategies:

1. **AI Ethics Boards**:

- o Create ethics boards to oversee AI projects and ensure compliance with ethical standards.
- o Example: Microsoft's AI and Ethics in Engineering and Research (AETHER) Committee.

2. **Regulatory Compliance**:

- o Ensure that AI systems comply with relevant laws and regulations.

o Example: Adhering to GDPR requirements for data protection and privacy.

3. **Audit and Monitoring**:

   o Regularly audit and monitor AI systems to ensure they perform as intended and address any issues that arise.

   o Example: Setting up real-time monitoring tools to track the performance of an AI-powered chatbot.

4. **Stakeholder Engagement**:

   o Engage with stakeholders, including users, employees, and communities, to understand their needs and concerns.

   o Example: Conducting surveys and focus groups to gather feedback on AI systems.

6. EDUCATION AND AWARENESS

Educating stakeholders about AI and its ethical implications ensures that the human factor is integrated into AI systems.

Strategies:

1. **AI Literacy**:

   o Provide training and resources to improve AI literacy among employees and users.

   o Example: Offering workshops on AI ethics and responsible AI practices.

2. **Public Awareness**:

   o Raise public awareness about the benefits and risks of AI.

- o Example: Launching campaigns to educate the public about AI-powered technologies.

3. **Interdisciplinary Collaboration**:

- o Foster collaboration between AI experts, ethicists, sociologists, and other stakeholders.
- o Example: Hosting interdisciplinary conferences to discuss the ethical implications of AI.

7. REAL-WORLD EXAMPLES OF ADDING THE HUMAN FACTOR IN AI

a. IBM Watson for Oncology:

- IBM's AI system assists doctors in diagnosing and treating cancer.
- **Human Factor**: Doctors review and approve AI-generated treatment recommendations, ensuring human oversight and accountability.

b. Google's AI for Social Good:

- Google uses AI to address global challenges, such as predicting floods and protecting wildlife.
- **Human Factor**: AI systems are designed with input from local communities and stakeholders to ensure they meet real-world needs.

c. Microsoft's AI for Accessibility:

- Microsoft develops AI tools to empower people with disabilities.
- **Human Factor**: AI systems are designed with input

from people with disabilities to ensure inclusivity and accessibility.

Adding the **human factor** to AI systems is essential to ensure that they are ethical, fair, and aligned with human values. By incorporating **human oversight, ethical design, empathy, collaborative AI, ethical governance,** and **education,** organizations can build AI systems that are trustworthy, transparent, and beneficial to society. These strategies ensure that AI technologies enhance human capabilities and decision-making rather than replace them.

Emerging Technologies and Future Challenges

AI EMERGING TECHNOLOGIES & GOVERNANCE

FUTURE CHALLENGES

I. KEY EMERGING AI TECHNOLOGIES

These cutting-edge AI advancements are pushing governance boundaries:

1. Generative AI & Multimodal Models

- **Examples**: GPT-5, Gemini Ultra, Claude 3 Opus
- **Governance Challenges**:
    - Content provenance (deepfake detection)
    - Copyright infringement risks
    - Psychological manipulation potential

Case: OpenAI's "DALL-E 3" now embeds C2PA metadata for traceability

2. Agentic AI Systems

193

- **Autonomous AI agents** that plan/execute complex tasks
- **Risks**:
  - Unintended goal misalignment
  - Uncontrollable cascading actions

Example: Google's "AutoRT" requires real-time human oversight protocols

3. Neuro-Symbolic AI

- Combines neural networks with symbolic reasoning
- **Governance Needs**:
  - Hybrid explainability standards
  - Knowledge base auditing

Implementation: IBM's "Neuro-Symbolic AI Toolkit" includes ethics guardrails

4. Edge AI

- **Decentralized AI** on IoT devices
- **Challenges**:
  - Model drift across devices
  - Federated learning security

Solution: NVIDIA's "EGX Edge Governance" monitors distributed AI

5. Quantum Machine Learning

- **Exponential speedups** for AI training
- **Emerging Risks**:
  - Breaking current encryption
  - Unforeseen optimization behaviors

Prep Work: NIST's Post-Quantum Cryptography Standard (2024)

II. FUTURE GOVERNANCE CHALLENGES

1. ADAPTIVE REGULATORY FRAMEWORKS

Problem: Static laws can't keep pace with AI evolution

Solution Approaches:

- **Dynamic compliance** (Singapore's "living" AI governance)
- **Sandbox environments** (UK's DRCF regulatory testbeds)

2. AI-HUMAN HYBRID SYSTEMS

Challenge: Governing systems where humans and AI co-decide

Example:

- **AI "copilots" in healthcare** requiring new malpractice frameworks
- **Solution:** Joint liability models being tested in EU

3. GLOBAL COORDINATION GAPS

Current State:

- 40+ countries with conflicting AI laws
  Emerging Models:
- **UN AI Advisory Body's** global certification system (2025 pilot)
- **G7's** cross-border AI governance protocols

4. AI Self-Governance

Paradox: Using AI to govern AI

Implementations:

- **Anthropic's Constitutional AI** (self-monitoring)
- **Google's "AI Guardians"** (real-time compliance checks)

5. Existential Risk Management

Focus Areas:

- **Alignment research** (OpenAI's Superalignment team)
- **Containment protocols** for AGI development
- **Kill switches** for frontier models (Anthropic's "Red Button")

III. Sector-Specific Future Challenges

Sector	Emerging Tech	Governance Hurdle
Healthcare	Nano-scale AI diagnostics	FDA validation at quantum scales
Finance	Autonomous AI traders	Flash crash prevention
Defense	Swarm intelligence	IHL compliance for AI collectives
Education	Lifelong learning AI	Bias in personalized curricula

---

IV. Strategic Preparedness Framework

1. Technology Monitoring

- Maintain **Emerging Tech Radar** (quarterly updates)
- *Tool*: MITRE's AI Tech Atlas

2. Governance Architecture

A[AI System] --> B{Governance Layer}

B --> C[Adaptive Policy Engine]

B --> D[Real-Time Monitoring]

B --> E[Auto-Compliance]

3. Future-Proof Workforce

- **New Roles Emerging**:
  - AI Governance Architects
  - Quantum Risk Officers
  - Neuro-Symbolic Ethics Specialists

4. Continuous Scenario Planning

- **Wargame Exercises**:
  - AGI containment drills
  - Cross-border AI incident response

V. CALL TO ACTION

Immediate Steps for Organizations:

1. **Upgrade monitoring** for generative AI risks
2. **Pilot agentic AI** with circuit breakers
3. **Join** WEF's AI Governance Alliance
4. **Train staff** on neuro-symbolic auditing

Long-Term Investments:

- Post-quantum cryptography migration
- AI self-governance R&D
- Global policy engagement

197

Emerging Trends in AI Governance: A Detailed Analysis

1. SECTOR-SPECIFIC AI GOVERNANCE STANDARDS

Why It Matters:

Different industries require tailored approaches due to varying risk profiles and regulatory environments.

HEALTHCARE AI GOVERNANCE

Key Standards:

- **FDA's AI/ML-Based SaMD Framework** (2023 Update)
    - Requires:
        - **Continuous Learning Protocols** for adaptive AI
        - **Demographic Representation** in validation datasets
    - *Example*: AI diagnostic tools must be tested across 15+ ethnic groups.

- **EU MDR (Medical Device Regulation)**
    - Classifies AI diagnostics as **Class IIb/III devices**
    - Mandates **clinical evaluation reports** and **post-market surveillance**

Tools for Compliance:

- **NVIDIA Clara** (synthetic data generation)
- **IBM Watson Health** (bias detection in medical imaging AI)

FINANCIAL SERVICES AI GOVERNANCE

Key Standards:

- **Basel Committee's AI Principles (2024)**
  - Mandates:
    - **Explainable AI** for credit scoring (SHAP/LIME integration)
    - **"Human-in-the-Loop"** for high-stakes decisions (e.g., loan denials)
  - *Example*: Capital One uses **ZestFinance ZAML** for fair lending compliance.
- **SEC's Algorithmic Trading Rules (2024)**
  - Requires **pre-trade risk controls** and **audit trails**

Tools for Compliance:

- **Fiddler AI** (real-time model monitoring)
- **SAS Fair Banking** (regulatory reporting automation)

DEFENSE & NATIONAL SECURITY AI GOVERNANCE

Key Standards:

- **NATO's AI Certification Framework (2025 Draft)**
  - Bans:

- Fully autonomous weapons without **human kill-chain oversight**
- Opaque battlefield decision-support systems
    - *Example*: Raytheon's missile defense AI includes **ethical circuit breakers**.
- **U.S. DoD's Responsible AI Strategy (2023)**
    - Requires **red teaming** for all operational AI systems

Tools for Compliance:

- **MITRE's ATLAS** (adversarial threat modeling)
- **Palantir's AIP** (governed deployment of classified AI)

2. GLOBAL ALIGNMENT EFFORTS IN AI GOVERNANCE

Why It Matters:

Fragmented regulations create compliance burdens for multinational AI deployments.

Key Initiatives

Initiative	Led By	Progress (2024)	Impact
G7 Hiroshima Process	Japan/EU	Common "high-risk" AI taxonomy	Standardized compliance reporting
UN AI Advisory Body	38 nations	Global AI Ethics Certification	UN-backed audit frameworks

		(2025 pilot)	
OECD.AI Policy Observatory	45 countries	Live regulatory mapping tool	Compare EU/US/China rules

Case Study:

- **Microsoft's "One Governance Model"** aligns with:
  - ○ EU AI Act (high-risk requirements)
  - ○ China's Generative AI Rules (content filters)
  - ○ U.S. NIST RMF (risk management)

Strategic Implications:

- **72% of Fortune 500** now use **OECD's tracker** to anticipate regulatory changes
- **"Brussels Effect" 2.0**: EU standards becoming global benchmarks

3. AUTOMATED GOVERNANCE TOOLS (AI MONITORING AI)

Why It Matters:

Manual governance can't scale with AI's exponential growth.

Cutting-Edge Solutions

Tool Type	Leading Products	Key Features
Bias Auto-Detection	IBM Fairness AutoAI, Google's What-If Tool	Real-time demographic disparity alerts
Regulatory	Holistic AI Auditor,	Auto-generates EU

Compliance	Credo AI	AI Act technical docs
Anomaly Detection	AWS AI Guardians, Fiddler AI	Detects model drift in <100ms

Implementation Example:

- **Goldman Sachs** reduced bias audit costs by **60%** using:
  - o **Automated PSI monitoring** (population stability index)
  - o **SHAP-based explanation engine** for regulators

Future Trend:

- **AI Guardians** will soon:
  - o Auto-block non-compliant model deployments
  - o Negotiate compliance across jurisdictions

4. QUANTUM AI GOVERNANCE (PREPARING FOR FUTURE SYSTEMS)

Why It Matters:

Quantum computing will break current encryption and enable unprecedented AI capabilities by 2030.

Preparatory Measures

1. **Post-Quantum Cryptography (PQC)**
   - o **NIST CRYSTALS-Kyber** standard (2024)
   - o *Action Item:* Google Cloud will migrate AI services to PQC by 2026
2. **Quantum Machine Learning Safeguards**
   - o **D-Wave's QAI Ethics Toolkit** models:

- Drug discovery acceleration (1000x faster trials)
- Portfolio optimization risks (market instability)

3. **Policy Sandboxes**
   - **UK National Quantum Centre** tests:
     - Governance of quantum neural networks
     - Entanglement-based data privacy

Corporate Readiness Examples:

- **IBM**: Appointed first **Quantum Risk Officer** in 2023
- **JPMorgan Chase**: Quantum-resistant AI fraud detection by 2027

Strategic Implementation Roadmap

For Enterprises

1. **Sector-Specific Action**
   - Healthcare: Implement **FDA's predetermined change control plans**
   - Finance: Adopt **CFPB's algorithmic explanation templates**

2. **Global Compliance**
   - Use **OECD.AI's matrix** to build "highest

common denominator" AI

3. **Automated Governance**
   - o Pilot **AWS AI Guardians** or **Microsoft Responsible AI Dashboard**
4. **Quantum Prep**
   - o Conduct **PQC inventory** by 2025
   - o Join **WEF's Quantum Governance Consortium**

For Governments

- Develop **adaptive legislation** (Singapore's "living" AI governance)
- Fund **red teaming programs** for frontier models
- Establish **bilateral AI governance pacts** (e.g., US-EU Trade and Technology Council)

Future Outlook (2025-2030)

- **2026**: Mandatory sector-specific certifications (e.g., "FDA-Cleared AI Engineer")
- **2028**: AI governance automation market to hit **$12B** (Gartner)
- **2030**: First **quantum AI governance laws** expected

GOVERNING THE AI REVOLUTION

As we stand at the precipice of an AI-driven future, one truth becomes undeniable: **the governance of artificial intelligence will determine whether it becomes humanity's greatest ally or its most formidable adversary.** The frameworks, policies, and ethical guardrails we establish today will shape the trajectory of AI for generations to come.

The Stakes Have Never Been Higher

AI is no longer a speculative technology—it is **rewiring economies, redefining warfare, and reshaping human identity**. From healthcare diagnostics that outpace human doctors to autonomous financial systems that control trillion-dollar markets, AI's influence is pervasive. Yet, with great power comes **even greater responsibility**.

The Pillars of Effective AI Governance

1. **Proactive, Not Reactive**
   - Waiting for disaster is not an option. The EU AI Act, U.S. Executive Orders, and global initiatives like the G7 Hiroshima Process show that **forward-thinking regulation is possible**.

2. **Ethics at the Core**
   - AI must serve humanity—not the other way around. Principles like **fairness, transparency, and accountability** cannot be afterthoughts.

205

3. **Global Coordination**

   o AI respects no borders. **The UN's AI Advisory Body and OECD's policy observatories** are critical steps toward **harmonized governance.**

4. **Adaptability**

   o AI evolves faster than laws. **Sandbox environments, automated compliance tools, and dynamic policy engines** will keep governance agile.

5. **Preparing for the Unthinkable**

   o Quantum AI, artificial general intelligence (AGI), and self-governing systems are coming. **We must build safeguards today for the existential risks of tomorrow.**

A Call to Action

This is not a challenge for policymakers alone. **Every stakeholder—governments, corporations, researchers, and citizens—must engage.**

- **For Leaders:** Implement **sector-specific governance** now—before crises force your hand.
- **For Technologists:** Design AI with **embedded ethics**, not just performance metrics.
- **For the Public:** Demand **transparency and accountability** from AI systems that shape your life.

The Choice Before Us

Will AI be a force that **lifts humanity to unprecedented heights**, or will it deepen inequalities, erode trust, and spiral beyond our control? **The answer lies in the governance choices we make today.**

The future of AI is still unwritten. Let us write it with wisdom, courage, and unwavering commitment to the greater good.

Final Thought

"We are the architects of our AI destiny. Build wisely."